S0-BFD-003

Marissa

Thanks for
being such a
champion for our
students.

Bill

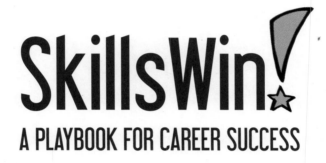

SkillsWin!

A PLAYBOOK FOR CAREER SUCCESS

Copyright © 2013 Sogna Entertainment, LLC

Hollywood • Dallas • Syracuse

To KC,
who keeps me company while the real magic happens!

Skills Win! A Playbook for CAREER Success

Copyright © 2013
Sogna Entertainment, LLC.
3907 Fredonia Dr, Suite 1/2
Hollywod, CA 90068
www.skillswin.com

Managing Editor and Interior Design by Michelle Sczpanski
Interior Design and Electronic Editing by Mackenzie Salmon
Edited by Sebastian Blanco and Erin McElroy
Cover Design © Sogna Designs
Cover Photograph © Sogna Designs

eBook edition created 2013.

All rights reserved. No part of this publication may be reproduced, stored in a retrieval
system, or transmitted in any form or by any means - electronic, mechanical,
photocopying, recording, or otherwise - without the prior written permission of
the publisher.

ISBN 978-0-578-12672-2

This book was printed in the United States of America by Sogna Designs.

SkillsWin!

A PLAYBOOK FOR CAREER SUCCESS

TABLE OF CONTENTS

FOREWARD

This Playbook has evolved over the past thirteen years starting with an emphasis of skills in my freshman course, leading to a book entitled, "10 Things Employers Want You to Learn in College," published by Ten Speed Press, and revised in a 2012 edition. Over that period a website was created to provide additional material on skills which was replaced by the Skills Win! website in 2013. Thousands of students have had the opportunity to use one of more of these products at the high school and college level. To all the Students, Teachers, Employers and members of audiences that I have addressed, thank you for your praise and your additions to the Skills Win! project.

While I initially conceived and drafted this Playbook, the efforts of Sebastian Blanco and Erin McElroy, to rebrand the 3cskills project, produce multimedia and social media content, in the form of an App and a completely new website, played a major role. In addition, Mackenzie Salmon worked as a graphic designer, developer of electronic material and copy editor of the book. Michelle Sczpanski served as managing editor, book designer and copy editor. Although both are college students, their work was good or better than many of the professional staffs I have worked with at major publishing houses.

I am ultimately responsible for the material in the book, but with this team, the book would have never been written and would not be near the quality it is.

INTRODUCTION

Coaches create playbooks to help their teams win games. This playbook can be your coach, guiding you towards a winning career. It provides you with an opportunity to improve chances of pursuing a great career path. It allows you to adjust to different opportunities you may encounter throughout your career, just like how coaches adjust plays based on other teams' defense during the season.

Skills Win!: A Playbook for Career Success is based on the idea that all careers require proficiency in the following 10 Skill Sets, which consist of 38 distinct skills.

We call this the *Skills Win! Playbook* for an obvious reason; you need to master each of these 10 Skill Sets in order to be successful in any career field. While these skills are not the only skills your future career might require you to master, they are relevant to everyday life. Don't make the mistake of thinking that if you already have the skills particular to the field of your choosing that you're too smart for this playbook. Merely knowing how to pull out a tooth doesn't make someone a good dentist. A dentist who is not a good time manager, is frequently hungover, fails to communicate clearly, can't send a clear email, can't sell an implant, doesn't keep good records, doesn't relate well to his employees or customers, who has trouble finding information on the Web, is number phobic, can't apply knowledge to figure out solutions to problems is going to fail, no matter how well he (or she) can pull out a tooth or fill a cavity.

This brief and action-oriented playbook is written for anyone who agrees that the following 10 Skill Sets are crucial for success:

1 Take Responsibility
2 Developing Physical Skills
3 Communicate Verbally
4 Communicate in Writing
5 Working Directly With People
6 Influencing People
7 Gathering Information
8 Use Quantitative Skills
9 Asking and Answering the Right Questions
10 Solving Problems

Tens of thousands of people have used these skills to achieve what they want for themselves, their families, and their communities.

Unfortunately, too many people are not aware that these 10 Skill Sets are the key to their success. Others are aware of some of these skills; yet they are not sure how to start developing them. Start practicing today so that you are equipped with a strong foundation, to have a successful career. Complete the exercises in this playbook, and you will succeed.

This playbook provides the tools that you need to be successful in whatever career path you might choose. What it will not give you is the will to practice and excel in the 10 Skill Sets. Mastering these skills is up to you. A playbook is not read like a novel or a textbook full of information. It serves as a starting point on the road to career success. Coaches don't ask their quarterbacks to simply curl up on the sofa and read over plays for the next big game—they expect their players to get up and practice! Like any athlete will tell you, success comes from practice and reflection. If you have the willingness to do what the playbook advises, I guarantee that you will be successful.

Consider this playbook your "personal skills trainer." As long as you are committed to showing up for practice, the playbook will be there to help you stay focused on developing your skills by providing activities to follow for each of the 38 skills.

LIKE ANY ATHLETE WILL TELL YOU, **success** COMES FROM **practice** AND **reflection**. IF YOU HAVE THE WILLINGNESS TO DO WHAT THE PLAYBOOK ADVISES, I **guarantee** THAT YOU WILL BE SUCCESSFUL."

– COPLIN, THE SKILLS PROFESSOR

HOW TO USE THE PLAYBOOK & IMPROVE ON ALL 38 SKILLS:

Each of the ten sections in the playbook will introduce you to the specific skills in the skill set. You will also be asked to complete a brief assessment of where you are on the 10 Skill Sets. This assessment will be used to generate your skill level score based on a scale of one-half star to five stars. Your goal should be to have five stars on all 10 Skill Sets. Next, the playbook will define and provide a short background definition on each of the skills within the set. Each of the 10 Skill Sets will address between three and six specific skills. For each skill, you will be asked to:

Return to the assessments after a few months of following your plan. If you have put forth a genuine effort to improving your skills, you will see enough improvement to raise your assessment score.

1 READ the definition and brief discussion on why the skill is important.

2 CIRCLE your current skill level and comment on why you assessed yourself that way.

3 REVIEW the Skills Win! Game Changers.

4 WRITE a plan on how you will improve your skills.

Ask yourself where you stand on a continuum between Homer Simpson, a lazy couch potato, and Richard Branson, one of the most successful people in the world. If you are closer to Simpson than Gates and you're okay with that, stop here. Don't fool yourself into thinking that you are ready for the Skills Win! Playbook; you would be better off using this playbook as coaster for your bottle of beer. If you are more like Gates, or if you're willing to do what it takes to become more like him, you're ready to do what this playbook tells you to do. If you reach five stars on at least eight of the 10 Skill Sets, you will be ready to "be all you can be" in whatever career field you pursue.

SKILL SET #1
TAKING RESPONSIBILITY

Taking responsibility is by far the most important of the 10 Skill Sets. You are not born a winner. Your parents, friends, teachers, mentors, or whomever else is in your life cannot give you all 38 skills from the 10 Skill Sets. They may help you practice and reflect on all those skills, but only you can decide to be a skills winner for yourself.

That means you cannot blame your lack of skills on anyone but yourself. Students or employees who mess up and then whine that assignments were not clear are playing the blame game. There is no more direct path to failure than failing to take responsibility for one's self.

People who are self-motivated, ethical in their

THERE IS NO MORE DIRECT PATH TO **FAILURE** THAN FAILING TO TAKE RESPONSIBILITY FOR ONE'S SELF.

dealings with others, and that manage both their time and their money well are winners. These people will easily find jobs because they do what needs to be done. People who need others to prod them, or who want a direct and immediate payoff for what they do are just like babies who cry at the slightest irritant. They also tend to be dishonest, frequently late, and usually have debt that they can't pay off. These people will struggle to succeed in the real world.

RUNDOWN >>
Taking responsibility consists of four skills:

#1 MOTIVATE YOURSELF
means working hard, showing enthusiasm, exceeding expectations, and continuously striving to improve oneself.

#2 BE ETHICAL
means telling the truth to yourself and others, complying with rules and regulations and fulfilling all commitments.

#3 MANAGE YOUR TIME
means completing all responsibilities well and on time.

#4 MANAGE YOUR MONEY
means making sure you are not spending more money than you are earning and that you are able to pay your debts.

SKILLS WIN! ASSESSMENT

Take the following assessment for Skill Set #1. Put a check in the box next to each question. Make sure you answer the questions honestly. If you lie, you are lying to yourself and probably will not succeed as you would like.

What would you do if your boss asks you to provide a report on a company that competes with you?
- ☐ 1. Cut and paste from the company website.
- ☐ 2. Look the company up on several websites and prepare a clear briefing.
- ☐ 3. In addition to the web research, call a friendly customer and ask what they think of the competitor.

How do you get yourself to do a task that you don't want to do?
- ☐ 1. Get it over as quickly and as soon as possible.
- ☐ 2. I promise myself a treat once the project is complete.
- ☐ 3. Do an excellent job on all important tasks.

What do you do if you take a job that you don't like?
- ☐ 1. Tell your friends and family how miserable you are.
- ☐ 2. Do enough not to get fired while you look for another job.
- ☐ 3. Work hard enough to get a raise and a promotion.

How often do you lie?
- ☐ 1. Never.
- ☐ 2. If it will help me achieve my goals.
- ☐ 3. Occasionally to avoid hurting people's feelings.

Under what conditions would you break a rule or regulation?
- ☐ 1. Never.
- ☐ 2. If I knew I would not get caught and it didn't hurt anyone.
- ☐ 3. If I could get permission of those who administer the rules.

If you were asked to make a commitment to do something that would further your career but were unsure you could make good on it, what would you do?
- ☐ 1. Make a commitment even if I was unsure I could keep it and then ask for an extension or reduction in the work required.
- ☐ 2. Ask for the deadline to be extended or the amount of work reduced before you accepted it.
- ☐ 3. Turn it down.

When you have many tasks to accomplish how do you decide what to work on?
- ☐ 1. I start with the first one on the list.
- ☐ 2. I take care of the ones requiring little time first.
- ☐ 3. I create an agenda with due dates and hours it will take.

Do you keep a schedule of everything you need to accomplish when given a task or multiple tasks?
- ☐ 1. I rarely make a schedule because it takes more time than it's worth.
- ☐ 2. I often make a schedule, but don't always refer to it.
- ☐ 3. Yes, I would be lost without one.

How often do you miss a deadline?
- ☐ 1. I ask for extensions sometimes and don't even meet those deadlines.
- ☐ 2. I don't like missing deadlines, but occasionally I miss one.
- ☐ 3. Never.

Do you know how much money you spent in the past month?
- ☐ 1. Yes, roughly.
- ☐ 2. I have a checkbook, but I check it against bank statements every 3 months.
- ☐ 3. Yes, I keep track of all my expenses and keep a budget that I check it against.

Think about your last big purchase. How did you decide what to spend?
- ☐ 1. I had just been paid so I knew I could afford it.
- ☐ 2. I am usually most concerned with getting a good price.
- ☐ 3. I determined how much I could afford and balanced that against the benefits.

Do you know when your next bill is due?
- ☐ 1. I do for big bills like rent and cell phone.
- ☐ 2. I just pay them as soon they come in if I have money in my checking account.
- ☐ 3. I maintain a list in an excel spreadsheet organized by due dates.

WHAT'S YOUR SKILLS WIN! SCORE?

Add the numbers you marked. See the table below to determine the number of stars.

Record your initial SkillsWin! assessment score here:

_____

It is recommended that you return and take the assessment every three months. Space is provided below for you to record your SkillsWin! assessment score.

DATE	SCORE
_____	_____
_____	_____
_____	_____
_____	_____

SKILL #1
MOTIVATE YOURSELF

Motivating yourself means working hard,
showing enthusiasm, exceeding expectations,
and continuously striving to improve oneself.

If I have to explain why motivation is the most critical of all skills in order to become a five star player on all of the 10 Skill Sets, then you are not in a good place. Laziness and a lack of work ethic will prevent you from developing the skill levels necessary to achieve your goals. These traits will not lead you to anywhere but a dead-end job, or even worse, no job at all. No pain, no gain! You don't necessarily need a five, but if you are not above a two, you are headed for a life of disappointment. The good news is, you are reading this Playbook and you are learning one for the most important skills. Now let's get started!

Here's a quick test to determine whether or not you can motivate yourself: did you do the assessment suggested on the previous page? If so, there is hope for you. If not, do it right now so that there can at least be some hope for you. If you don't before you read further, you are headed down the street of losers! and you are at home with Homer Simpson.

BE A WINNER!

Matt had a summer internship with a political group that took more interns than they needed. Instead of sitting and complaining that he was bored like the other interns, Matt asked if he could help make copies. After about 10,000 copies, his superiors put him in charge of an important project and asked him to start managing the other ten cry-baby interns.

LAZINESS AND
A LACK OF WORK ETHIC
WILL PREVENT YOU FROM
DEVELOPING THE SKILL LEVELS
NECESSARY TO ACHIEVE YOUR GOALS.

THINK ABOUT IT

How well do you motivate yourself? Circle your score.

1   **2**   **3**   **4**   **5**

POOR   OUTSTANDING

Comment on why you gave yourself this score here:

_____

_____

_____

_____

GAME CHANGERS

1 Set a goal for yourself. Identify the steps needed to reach the goal and indicate a deadline for each step.

2 Get up an hour before you usually do and get some work done for five straight days.

3 Reward your efforts by doing something you enjoy after completing each step of your goal.

MAKE A SKILL IMPROVEMENT PLAN

Describe and give examples of how you plan to improve or maintain your self-motivation.

_____

_____

_____

_____

_____

_____

SKILL #2
BE ETHICAL

Being ethical means telling the truth to yourself and others, complying with rules and regulations, and fulfilling all commitments you make.

Thinking about the ethical consequences of your actions is a crucial step to success. You may not think to ask yourself if you are doing the right thing or if are you are telling the truth when you are pressed for time and stressed. Sometimes the right answer is not obvious, and it might raise questions about things that you would prefer not to think about. Get over it. Make a habit of asking someone you respect what they think about what you are saying and doing. Would you want to tell them about some action you took that you may not think is ethical after you did it? This is a good test.

Aside from the fact that you should be ethical because it is the right thing to do, being ethical is also key to a successful career. If your co-workers or supervisors sometimes doubt that you are telling the truth, or if you take actions that you know may not be acceptable to those in authority, you will lose their trust. Trust can be lost very quickly, and once trust is lost, it is almost impossible to get back. Losing trust means you will not be asked to do more or take on bigger responsibilities that could help you advance further.

BE A WINNER!

Linda got a high-paying job with a top company after graduation. She was well-liked and on the path towards a promotion. Later it was discovered that Linda padded her expense account on a business trip, and she was fired. She also had trouble getting another job because employers wanted to know why she left such a good job with such a good company. Do you think she should have told the new employer that she was fired for cheating on her expense account?

THINK ABOUT IT

How ethical are you? Circle your score.

1 **2** **3** **4** **5**

POOR   OUTSTANDING

Comment on why you gave yourself this score here:

_____

_____

_____

_____

GAME CHANGERS

1 Never make a promise you can't keep. Always hold yourself to your word.

2 Next time you make a decision, first ask yourself: "What would my mother think of this choice?"

3 "Treat others the way you want to be treated." Remember this golden rule and practice it daily.

MAKE A SKILL IMPROVEMENT PLAN

Describe and give examples of how you plan to improve or maintain your ethical behavior when dealing with others.

_____

_____

_____

_____

_____

_____

SKILL #3
MANAGE YOUR TIME

Managing your time means completing all responsibilities well and on time.

Good time management is absolutely essential for career success. Time management is essential to meeting deadlines successfully. Knowing and meeting your deadlines will save you time and money. You will be faced with many tasks that require different levels of work due at different times. Keeping deadlines will prevent you from falling behind, which makes it easier to meet future deadlines. Good time management also makes it easier to accommodate unexpected events, which means avoiding finishing a task at the last minute.

Don't fall for the procrastinator's lie and tell yourself that you will work more efficiently against a deadline. This attitude will lead you to miss a deadline eventually. While turning a paper in late at school may cost you 5% of your grade, coming late to an important meeting or turning in a report late could cost you your job. Make the commitment to never turn in anything late now so that you can be a more effective time manager in the future.

BE A WINNER!

College students frequently miss deadlines because they are poor time managers. Sometimes this leads to students getting D's or F's, but usually not. As a result of this weak punishment, college students are trained to miss deadlines. This habit will not work in the work world. Ultimately, it will lead to poor performance reviews that will cost you money or your job and career.

> MAKE THE COMMITMENT TO NEVER TURN IN ANYTHING LATE **NOW** SO THAT YOU CAN BE A MORE EFFECTIVE TIME MANAGER IN THE FUTURE.

Most people have the biggest problem managing their time when it comes to large projects with distant deadlines. The best way to handle these big projects is to create a list of steps that must be completed and to estimate how long they will take. Block out periods on a calendar (days and hours) when you complete each step. Give yourself plenty of extra time in your plans for illness, computer problems and lack of help from others.

THINK ABOUT IT

How well do you manage your time? Circle your score.

1   **2**   **3**   **4**   **5**

POOR   OUTSTANDING

Comment on why you gave yourself this score here:

_____

_____

_____

_____

GAME CHANGERS

1 Make a list of tasks to be completed each day, then rank each task in order of importance.

2 Use a planner to keep track of all appointments and assignments.

3 Show up five minutes early to all meetings, appointments, or classes.

MAKE A SKILL IMPROVEMENT PLAN

Describe and give examples of how you plan to improve or maintain your time management.

_____

_____

_____

_____

_____

_____

SKILL #4
MANAGE YOUR MONEY

Managing your money means not spending more money than you are earning and that you are able to pay your debts with no late payments.

The ability to limit expenditures so that your income exceeds your expenses is a critical skill for career success. It means that you must make responsible financial decisions given your resources. Every job requires you to allocate your time and effort in a way that leads to good job performance. Moreover, money problems can affect your attention to your job. Calls from bill collectors raise stress, which can lead to mistakes on crucial job related details. Good money management indicates how organized you are and whether or not you can act in your own interest.

There are two very simple ways to stop increasing your debt. First, reduce your expenditures by buying only what you need, not want. Second, increase the amount of money you earn. The second may not be so easy.

There may be a time when you need to take on

BIG NUMBER
$15,950

The average American household with at least one credit card and carries an average of $15,950. Don't let credit cards trick you in to spending above your means by using it to pay for things you use quickly, like meals or shopping. Put aside cash instead so that you can cover your bill's balance in full each month.

REDUCE YOUR EXPENDITURES BY BUYING ONLY WHAT YOU **NEED**, NOT WANT.

debt for large expenditures like a college education, a house, or a car. Always think of ways to minimize these kinds of debt. Don't be like the college students who tell me that they will graduate with $70,000 in debt, and they plan to take a summer overseas that will cost another $5,000.

THINK ABOUT IT

How well do you manage your money? Circle your score.

1   **2**   **3**   **4**   **5**

POOR   OUTSTANDING

Comment on why you gave yourself this score here:

_____

_____

_____

_____

GAME CHANGERS

1 Make a budget for yourself this month that allows money for entertainment, clothes, food, transportation, etc. Keep track of receipts to help you stick to your budget.

2 Learn how to balance a checkbook and be sure to do so every month.

3 Use a computer-based tool such as Microsoft Money or Quicken on your own finances.

MAKE A SKILL IMPROVEMENT PLAN

Describe and give examples of how you plan to improve or maintain your money management.

_____

_____

_____

_____

_____

_____

SKILL SET #2
DEVELOPING PHYSICAL SKILLS

Physical skills are not always at the top of everyone's list of skills required for career success, but they should be. This list of four physical skills advises you on the four most essential physical skills that you need to master to be successful in your career.

Developing these skills can be difficult. Your physical makeup can limit your health, your appearance, your typing, and even your handwriting. There is only so much that some people can do about these traits given their individual ability, but everyone has room to improve upon these skills to the best of their ability no matter their current skill-level.

It may be hard and time-consuming, but making a commitment to practice and reflect on these skills can increase your performance at work substantially. You'll find that others are much more likely to treat you like a professional from the start when your physical appearance, handwriting, and typing all demonstrate that you are professional.

Developing skills can not only help you make the best first impression possible in a job interview or a workplace setting, but it can also help you improve your self-confidence. Showing that you are competent in these four skills will prove to others that you are a winner, which is one of the first and most important steps towards a successful career.

RUNDOWN >>

Developing physical skills consists of four skills:

#5 STAY WELL means having the mental alertness and physical energy necessary to complete tasks to the best of one's ability.

#6 LOOK GOOD is defined as presenting a professional appearance.

#7 TYPE WELL is defined as typing a minimum of 35 words per minute on a computer keyboard mistake-free.

#8 WRITE LEGIBLY is defined as recording or summarizing relevant information, read or heard, in a form that you will be able to use later.

SKILL SET #2
SKILLS WIN! ASSESSMENT

Take the following assessment for Skill Set #2. Put a check in the box next to each question. Make sure you answer the questions honestly. If you lie, you are lying to yourself and probably will not succeed as you would like.

Do you exercise on a regular basis?
☐ 1. I hardly ever work out, but stay active.
☐ 2. I do some running three times a week.
☐ 3. I make sure I have a long quick paced walk or work out every day.

How often do you feel too tired to concentrate at work?
☐ 1. A few times per month.
☐ 2. Only on Mondays and Fridays.
☐ 3. Never?

Do you consider yourself a healthy eater?
☐ 1. I pretty much eat whatever I like.
☐ 2. I eat a good breakfast, but sometimes eat a snack if I don't have time for a meal.
☐ 3. I make sure to keep a balanced diet and keep away from snack foods.

If you are invited to attend and event do you ask for the dress code?
☐ 1. I assume everyone is going to be casual.
☐ 2. Usually, I would wear what I would wear to work.
☐ 3. Of course I would ask for the dress code, you don't want to show up underdressed.

Do you take pride in your appearance when getting ready for the day?
☐ 1. I would rather be comfortable than anything else.
☐ 2. I try to look presentable.
☐ 3. I make sure to give myself enough time each morning so I don't rush to get ready.

If you were asked to attend an interview tomorrow, would you have something to wear?
☐ 1. I'm sure I could find something buried in my closet.
☐ 2. I'm not sure what you're supposed to wear for an interview.
☐ 3. Yes, several options.

Have you ever practiced and timed your typing adjusting for errors?
☐ 1. Never.
☐ 2. A long time ago and I remember I typed at least 35 wpm adjusted for no errors.
☐ 3. Yes, about once a year and I practice if my speed has dropped.

How fast can you type adjusted for no errors?
☐ 1. Less than 15 words-per-minute.
☐ 2. 25 word-per-minute with few errors.
☐ 3. 45 words-per-minute or more, error free.

Do you look at your fingers when you type?
☐ 1. Always.
☐ 2. Sometimes especially for numbers.
☐ 3. Never.

Are you asked to clarify your handwriting frequently?
☐ 1. Most of the time.
☐ 2. Sometimes.
☐ 3. Never.

Do you take notes in a systematic or orderly fashion?

- ☐ 1. I never take notes.
- ☐ 2. I write down a few key dates or points, but not much else.
- ☐ 3. People frequently ask for my notes after meetings.

Do you use shorthand when taking notes if the dictation is too fast?

- ☐ 1. I don't know shorthand.
- ☐ 2. I use my own version of shorthand and then re-write the notes later.
- ☐ 3. I have take a shorthand class and found it very beneficial to use during meetings.

WHAT'S YOUR SKILLS WIN! SCORE?

Add the numbers you marked. See the table below to determine the number of stars.

.5	1	1.5	2	2.5	3	3.5	4	4.5	5
12-14	15-17	18-20	21-23	24-26	27-28	29-30	31-32	33-34	32-36

Record your initial SkillsWin! assessment score here:

_____

It is recommended that you return and take the assessment every three months. Space is provided below for you to record your SkillsWin! assessment score.

DATE   **SCORE**

_____   _____

_____   _____

_____   _____

_____   _____

SKILL #5
STAY WELL

Staying well means having the mental alertness and physical energy necessary to complete tasks to the best of one's ability.

It is hard to achieve long-term success in a job without making a long-term commitment to staying healthy. "Alertness" is a word frequently used in interviews and published lists of characteristics of a good worker, but a person who is regularly ill may find it difficult to focus on their tasks.

BE A WINNER!

Beyond living a healthy lifestyle, it is important to remember that consuming drugs and alcohol is a major threat to career success for many people. Coming to work hungover may seem funny or glamorous in the movies, but in reality substance use (not just abuse) can have a negative effect on your ability to perform well at your job, and raises your risk of getting fired. Even worse, getting busted for alcohol or drugs could result in a criminal record, which will follow you for many years. Having substance abuse charges on your record also makes you ineligible for many jobs, especially those in government.

Those who maintain good health are more likely to have higher grades and a greater capacity to undertake leadership positions during college, which employers appreciate. Good health is also a positive quality to bring up in a job interview.

No one likes being sick, but frequent illness leading to regular absence from work or school is seen as a red flag to employers during job interviews. Even though employers will not ask about personal matters such as health, it is something on their minds.

Having a poor attendance record due to illnesses can been avoided through common-sense practices like eating right, exercising, sleeping well, and washing your hands.

THINK ABOUT IT

How well do you prioritize staying well? Circle your score.

1   **2**   **3**   **4**   **5**

POOR   OUTSTANDING

Comment on why you gave yourself this score here:

_____

_____

_____

_____

GAME CHANGERS

1 Go to sleep and wake up at the same time each day.

2 Drink eight glasses of water per day.

3 Find a gym buddy who will workout with you at least three times a week.

MAKE A SKILL IMPROVEMENT PLAN

Describe and give examples of how you plan to improve or maintain your commitment to staying well.

_____

_____

_____

_____

_____

SKILL #6
LOOK GOOD

Looking good means presenting a professional appearance.

Looking good means being well groomed. Not everyone is born looking like a movie star, and that's okay. However, the amount of effort that you put into making yourself presentable says a lot about your character. Your appearance communicates a lot about who you are, and you must decide what you want it to say about you. Dressing well shows the people around you that you care about yourself and take pride in how others see you. This means that you are also much more likely to take pride in your work, which is a very important quality for employers looking to hire someone.

Maintaining a professional appearance is an essential part of achieving success in the workplace. If you come to a job interview or work smelling bad, having messy hair, or wearing clothes you pulled out of the laundry bag without ironing, you show a lack of respect for both yourself and those around you. Employers need people who are able to represent their company to clients and other companies. Any boss is going to be reluctant to hire someone to represent a company or organization if he or she is unable to dress appropriately.

What exactly does "professional" mean when it comes to attire for your specific line of work? The best advice is to dress like those in the workforce who are at least five years older than you. Always ask if you are unsure of the dress code for a job interview or work-related activity. Failing to do so could cost you the job.

BE A WINNER!

Research shows that first impressions are formed in less than a minute. Unless you meet someone on the phone or through email, that person will form an impression of you based on your physical appearance before you even have a chance to open your mouth. What will they see? Enough said!

THINK ABOUT IT

How well do you prioritize staying well? Circle your score.

1   **2**   **3**   **4**   **5**

POOR   OUTSTANDING

Comment on why you gave yourself this score here:

_____

_____

_____

_____

GAME CHANGERS

1 Practice sitting up straight during your next meal.

2 Model yourself after professionals you observe.

3 Dress how you would like to be treated.

MAKE A SKILL IMPROVEMENT PLAN

Describe and give examples of how you plan to improve or maintain your professional appearance.

_____

_____

_____

_____

_____

_____

SKILL #7
TYPE WELL

Typing well means typing a minimum of 35 words per minute on a computer keyboard mistake-free.

One of the reasons that fast and accurate typing is important is that you will have to write reports in almost any job. Gone are the days of typewriters—and of secretaries and typing pools who will transcribe your reports for you. Highly paid professionals do their own typing. Analysts who are paid $200,000 per year by consulting companies don't have their own secretaries to type their reports. The faster and more accurately you can type, the better off you will be.

Typing quickly and accurately will also open many doors for you for initial jobs and advancement. Good word processors can be hired for between $10 and $20 an hour through "temp" firms, but you must be able to type 45 words per minute at minimum in order to be hired by these firms.

Good typing will enable you to be a team leader without the awkwardness of having to ask for the position. Being the one at the computer in a team allows you to filter your teammates' ideas as you type, which virtually puts you in control of the team.

Typing may seem like an obvious skill, given how much today's society relies on computers and other technology. However, you might be surprised to find out how many people struggle with typing quickly and accurately. Today's technology with smartphones has confused people over what is typing. It is not hunting and pecking with a finger or a stylus, nor is it typing emails with special short words. Learning how to type does not apply only to writing, but also to entering data as well. Every time I mention the typing skill in a speech or lecture, people in the audience come up and say something similar to what a teacher once told me, "I never took a typing class, and it takes me four hours to write a four- or five-page report." Don't let that happen to you.

BIG NUMBER

2 YEARS

Want to retire early? You could save two years of your working life by learning to type 50 words per minute versus 25 words per minute.

34

THINK ABOUT IT

How well do you prioritize typing well? Circle your score.

1   **2**   **3**   **4**   **5**

POOR   OUTSTANDING

Comment on why you gave yourself this score here:

_____

_____

_____

_____

GAME CHANGERS

1 Turn off your Internet and take notes in class on your computer.

2 Do not look at your fingers when you type.

3 Take a computer based typing test once a month to track your speed improvements.

MAKE A SKILL IMPROVEMENT PLAN

Describe and give examples of how you plan to improve or maintain your typing.

_____

_____

_____

_____

_____

_____

SKILL #8
WRITE LEGIBLY

Writing legibly means recording or summarizing relevant information, read or heard, in a form that you will be able to use later.

Having good handwriting and being able to take decipherable notes quickly is a valuable asset. Aside from allowing you to have a good personal record of what happened at any meeting, good notes can be used to influence future meetings and events. You can present what you have recorded faithfully but still organize the information in a way that helps express your point of view.

Don't think you don't need to write legibly because you can take your laptop or tablet to a meeting. If the meeting is with company big wigs, they will tell you to get off your computer. You don't want to start off on the wrong foot with your bosses simply because you can't read your own handwriting.

Another big advantage of having clear handwriting is that it enables you to write professional-looking thank-you notes every time you go on an interview. A readable note that looks as if it were written by an adult and not by a child or medical doctor (who are notorious for unreadable prescriptions) works wonders. An email or typed letter just won't do it. Employers and alums who serve as mentors tell me how much they appreciate receiving notes. Receiving a short note from students for whom I've written a letter of recommendation makes me want to write more letters for them in the future.

BE A WINNER!

Good handwriting might seem like a skill that has gone out of style these days given how much people rely on computers to send e-mails and write reports. However, good handwriting is a very important skill to have. Many times you will find yourself in situations like meetings that require you to take written notes. Don't be the person who isn't able to read his own writing after the fact.

THINK ABOUT IT

How well do you prioritize staying well? Circle your score.

1   **2**   **3**   **4**   **5**

POOR   OUTSTANDING

Comment on why you gave yourself this score here:

_____

_____

_____

_____

GAME CHANGERS

1 Never attend a meeting without taking written notes.

2 Label all of the notes you take. At minimum, write the subject and the date on the top of each page of notes.

3 Gr8 note taking is a balance b/w legibility & content, so don't b afraid 2 use abrevs once in a while.

MAKE A SKILL IMPROVEMENT PLAN

Describe and give clear examples of how you plan to improve or maintain your penmanship.

_____

_____

_____

_____

_____

_____

SKILL SET #3
COMMUNICATING VERBALLY

Verbal communication is a formal term for talking and listening. Some people are good talkers and some are good listeners, but you need to be good at both. Good verbal communication is necessary in order to arrive at a mutual understanding. Talking in an informal conversation is very different from speaking to groups.

The skills in this Skill Set are important because they function as building blocks for Skill Set 5, Working Directly With People and Skill Set 6, Influencing Others. If you are skilled at establishing trust and cooperating with others, you will have an easier time communicating verbally. Similarly, you will find it much easier to persuade other people to adopt your ideas if you can effectively communicate your ideas with others in one-on-one conversations and presentations.

These three Skill Sets complement each other, but they can also be developed independently. People who consider themselves shy may find practicing these skills intimidating at first. However, overcoming those fears will pay off in the long run. People who communicate well will find that it is much easier to advance in the workplace and achieve both short and long-term goals when they present their ideas clearly and establish strong relationships with others.

RUNDOWN >>

Communicating verbally consists of three skills:

#9 CONVERSE ONE-ON-ONE
means conveying ideas and sharing thoughts with another person.

#10 PRESENT TO GROUPS
means speaking clearly, confidently, and concisely to others.

#11 USE VISUAL DISPLAYS
means presenting your ideas well through charts, illustrations, diagrams and images.

SKILL SET #3
SKILLS WIN! ASSESSMENT

Take the following assessment for Skill Set #3. Put a check in the box next to each question. Make sure you answer the questions honestly. If you lie, you are lying to yourself and probably will not succeed as you would like.

Do you think about how clearly you speak in terms of speed and loudness to someone in a professional setting?
- ☐ 1. I just talk the way I usually do.
- ☐ 2. I assume the people I am talking to will let me know if they can't hear or understand me.
- ☐ 3. I am conscious of the need to project my voice and not talk too fast.

When talking to someone how do you make sure you both have the same understanding?
- ☐ 1. Most of the time I just assume we understand each other.
- ☐ 2. I speak clearly and repeat myself.
- ☐ 3. Asking questions is the best way to make sure I understand and the other person understands me.

Do you dominate the conversation or let others have time to speak?
- ☐ 1. I take the time I need to get my point across.
- ☐ 2. Sometimes I get carried away and dominate the conversation.
- ☐ 3. I like to let the other person talk as much as possible and I listen carefully.

When giving a presentation do you maintain eye contact with your audience?
- ☐ 1. It makes me nervous, so I try to avoid other people's gaze.
- ☐ 2. I will occasionally make eye contact with someone in the audience.
- ☐ 3. Always, it helps keep the audience engaged and I make sure to look at different people in the audience.

How many times do you practice a presentation before giving it?
- ☐ 1. I wing it. I work better on the spot.
- ☐ 2. Usually once, right before the presentation to remind myself of the information.
- ☐ 3. Several times to make sure I'm keeping a good pace and communicating clearly.

How well do you answer questions during a presentation?
- ☐ 1. I don't usually finish in time to allow for questions.
- ☐ 2. I try to give them as much information as possible in my response.
- ☐ 3. I take a moment to compile my thoughts, answer the questions and then ask if they need more clarification.

When giving a presentation what sorts of visual aids do you use?
- ☐ 1. I don't use visual aids.
- ☐ 2. I usually have a slide show or PowerPoint going in the background.
- ☐ 3. I use PowerPoint and/or handouts to help the audience follow along.

Do you consider design when creating your visual displays?
- ☐ 1. I'd rather focus on getting the information across rather than the way it looks.
- ☐ 2. Yes, having a visually appealing presentation is as important as the information provided.
- ☐ 3. I use a design that minimizes the number of words used and high lights the important points.

When presenting, do you read from your visual displays?

☐ 1. My PowerPoint is like my script.
☐ 2. I tend to rely too heavily on my displays, but I'm trying to get better.
☐ 3. I try not to repeat what is on the displays, but assume the audience is processing it and I am helping people to understand my point.

WHAT'S YOUR SKILLS WIN! SCORE?

Add the numbers you marked. See the table below to determine the number of stars.

.5	1	1.5	2	2.5	3	3.5	4	4.5	5
12-14	15-17	18-20	21-23	24-26	27-28	29-30	31-32	33-34	32-36

Record your initial SkillsWin! assessment score here:

_____

It is recommended that you return and take the assessment every three months. Space is provided below for you to record your SkillsWin! assessment score.

DATE   **SCORE**

_____   _____

_____   _____

_____   _____

_____   _____

SKILL #9
CONVERSE ONE-ON-ONE

Conversing one-on-one means conveying ideas and sharing thoughts with another person.

Having a conversation with someone, whether in a job setting or elsewhere, requires both talking and listening. Communication is a two-way street and can only be effective if your interest in talking is equal to your ability to be a good listener. In fact, most experts say that listening is more important than talking in good communications, which is why you have probably heard the saying "God gave you two ears and one mouth."

Your style of speaking and the clarity with which you speak are just as important as using correct grammar. It's also important to think about the way you organize your conversation. Remember to stick to the point and not wander all over the place. In short, you need to be precise about what information you are trying to provide and what information you are trying to receive.

Mutual understanding through good verbal communication in the work world is vital. Misunderstandings can lead to disasters in dealing with customers and coworkers. If you cannot understand what your boss wants you to do, you have the choice of asking for clarification or doing the wrong thing. The former is better, but getting it right the first time is the best. A senior human resource person writes, "I think conversing one-on-one is my main skill set. A new-hire must be able to carry a conversation—willing to learn. The training process that all our new-hires must complete can be very confusing, and we expect each new-hire to ask questions in order to grasp a full understanding. If someone cannot hold a decent conversation, I am hesitant to even place them in a lower-end job, even if they have the education and training."

BE A WINNER!

Just answer the question. Next time you ask someone something or someone asks you something, see if the question is answered directly. When asked a yes or no question, people sometimes justify the answer without giving the answer. If your boss asks you if you have finished the report, you may want to give an excuse in stead of saying "No, I haven't." You learned to do this when your mother asked, "Did you take out the trash?" and you tell her how busy you have been. Your boss is not your mother.

THINK ABOUT IT

How well do you converse one-on-one? Circle your score.

1   2   3   4   5

POOR   OUTSTANDING

Comment on why you gave yourself this score here:

_____

_____

_____

_____

GAME CHANGERS

1 Explain directions to your local grocery store to a stranger.

2 Call a relative or friend who you have not spoken with in awhile and have a conversation for at least 10 minutes.

3 Find a professional who works in the field you are interested in and ask them to tell you about their work.

MAKE A SKILL IMPROVEMENT PLAN

Describe and give examples of how you plan to improve or maintain your ability to converse one-on-one.

_____

_____

_____

_____

_____

_____

PRESENT TO GROUPS

Presenting to groups means speaking clearly, confidently, and concisely to others.

Talking to groups means presenting and listening to any number of people, ranging from a few to thousands! The techniques that you use will vary depending on the size of the group, and they are essentially different from one-on-one conversations. Successful group presentations require you to find out if you are getting your message across. Before you give a speech, learn to ask yourself, "How will I know if my talk has been successful?" After the speech, take some time to reflect and see if you passed your own test. Did you stay on task and talk at a reasonable pace? Did you make eye contact with different people in the room? Did you receive good questions and give clear answers? If not, ask yourself how you can improve the next time you speak.

It is also essential to not be fearful of a crowd in order to be an effective public speaker. Some people who do very heroic things get sweaty palms and become speechless when placed in front of a group. The size is not always the determining factor. Some people can handle speaking to a group of a couple of hundred strangers well, but instantly get nervous in front of a group of ten coworkers. It can be hard to learn to get over stage fright, but the only way to overcome it is to practice.

BE A WINNER!

Remember to respect your audience's time when giving a speech or presentation. No one wants to listen to a speaker that goes on for too long, no matter how interesting your topic might be. You risk losing your audience's attention and being remembered as boring. Find out how much time you have to present and practice your speech or presentation several times beforehand to make sure you can stay on time. Your audience will thank you.

THINK ABOUT IT

How well do you present to groups? Circle your score.

1　　**2**　　**3**　　**4**　　**5**
POOR　　　　　　　　　　　　　OUTSTANDING

Comment on why you gave yourself this score here:

_____

_____

_____

_____

GAME CHANGERS

1 Participate in activities that require you to make formal and informal presentations.

2 Look at the audience and count to ten before you start talking.

3 Practice having energetic body language and speaking in an upbeat tone of voice the next time you give a presentation.

MAKE A SKILL IMPROVEMENT PLAN

Describe and give examples of how you plan to improve or maintain your ability to present to groups.

_____

_____

_____

_____

_____

_____

SKILL #11
USE VISUAL DISPLAYS

Using visual displays means clearly presenting your ideas through charts, illustrations, diagrams, and images.

A visual display does not necessarily mean a fancy PowerPoint presentation. It can be a single sheet of paper handed out to the group that outlines the topics you plan to discuss. You may not need to make a PowerPoint for everything, but you do need to become proficient in using PowerPoint, as well as creating visual displays on handouts, overheads, or newsprint-like papers that you place on the wall. Don't try to dump everything you want to say in a single slide.

Visual displays are always crucial when you speak to a group. Visual displays, by definition, help you move from simply telling the audience to showing them. By asking your audience to react to a chart or a diagram, you involve them in the speech, which will naturally keep them more interested.

In order to use visual displays effectively you need to master your topic and organize your content well enough to integrate a display into your talk. You also need to produce the display, which could be anything from simple layouts on an 8½ by 11 piece of paper to a PowerPoint presentation. The first task always defines the second.

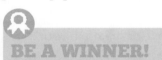

BE A WINNER!

Don't underestimate the value of a paper handout. Often times an effective handout can work as a visual aid as well as a PowerPoint. You should provide your audience a copy of your PowerPoint presentation in some paper form so they can take notes. It will make you look like you really have your act together.

Most of the people you will be working for will not have the skills to take care of displays. Even if they do, they might not have the time. Your display-making skills will make you indispensable. Just be careful to avoid being labeled as someone who can only create displays. The best way to avoid such a label is to make substantive suggestions about improving the content of presentations. This shows your superiors you are ready for more responsibility.

If you are making a presentation using a set of PowerPoint slides, avoid reading directly from the slides. This is a common mistake made by far too many speakers. Assume the audience can read and elaborate on one or more of the points on the slide.

THINK ABOUT IT

How well do you use visual displays? Circle your score.

1 **2** **3** **4** **5**

POOR   OUTSTANDING

Comment on why you gave yourself this score here:

_____

_____

_____

_____

GAME CHANGERS

1 Use paper handouts at the next meeting in which you present.

2 Create a PowerPoint using an interactive presentation program like Prezi.

3 Less is more when it comes to PowerPoint presentations. Limit yourself to three lines of text per slide.

MAKE A SKILL IMPROVEMENT PLAN

Describe and give examples of how you plan to improve or maintain your ability to use visual displays.

_____

_____

_____

_____

_____

_____

SKILL SET #4
COMMUNICATING IN WRITING

The purpose of written communication is the same as that of oral communication: promoting mutual understanding between two or more people. If you were considered a bad writer by your teachers in high school, college or even graduate school, it does not mean that you are doomed to be one in your career. The same goes if your teachers told you that you were a good writer.

The writing that you will likely find yourself doing in your career is very different from the writing that you did as a student. Academic writing may have purposes, like self-exploration, developing ideas, or just filling space. Writing in your career is about communicating specific information and viewpoints clearly with as few words as possible. You may have tried to write as much as possible to meet word requirements or page requirements when writing papers for class, but be warned that writing less is better in the real world.

Your boss does not want to have to read any more unnecessary words than they have to, and they will also expect the work that you do to be free of spelling or grammatical errors. In addition, selective use of bold, italics, and other formatting, and bullets can help order and convey a message more effectively. Always remember to take the time to carefully review and edit your work, and remember that the less ink you use, the better.

RUNDOWN >>

Communicating in writing consists of four skills:

#12 WRITE WELL means effectively communicating, using text in order to convey one's ideas, knowledge, and opinions.

#13 EDIT AND PROOF means frequently reviewing and correcting mistakes in one's work.

#14 USE WORD PROCESSING TOOLS means operating basic word processing programs, and their features for different types of products.

#15 MASTER ONLINE COMMUNICATION means using email and other electronic-based mediums to send and receive messages with proper etiquette.

SKILLS WIN! ASSESSMENT

Take the following assessment for Skill Set #4. Put a check in the box next to each question. Make sure you answer the questions honestly. If you lie, you are lying to yourself and probably will not succeed as you would like.

Do you have experience writing memos, grants or technical manuals?
- ☐ 1. Except for emails and things for professors, I never write.
- ☐ 2. I have written several memos as part of my job, but just to my boss.
- ☐ 3. Yes, I often have to write one or two page memos for distribution to several people and received positive responses.

When you want to write an email, letter, report or memo, how do you begin?
- ☐ 1. I just start writing.
- ☐ 2. I gather all my information and start with an introduction.
- ☐ 3. First, I establish the goal of the assignment then create an outline.

Do you have trouble staying within a word count?
- ☐ 1. All of the time.
- ☐ 2. Sometimes, but I try to be as concise as possible.
- ☐ 3. The less ink the better even though it takes more time.

Do you read your written work, including emails, before sending or submitting them?
- ☐ 1. Rarely
- ☐ 2. I skim them over quickly to check for major errors.
- ☐ 3. I always read through anything I've written completely to check for errors.

Have you ever read *The Elements of Style* by William Strunk Jr. and E.B. White or some other writing guide?
- ☐ 1. Never.
- ☐ 2. Not since high school.
- ☐ 3. I have a copy at my desk so I can reference it when needed.

How do you distinguish between editing and proofing?
- ☐ 1. I don't. They are basically the same task.
- ☐ 2. Editing requires getting grammar mistakes while proofing means checking for typos and spelling mistakes.
- ☐ 3. Editing requires looking at the organization of paragraphs and sentences as well as the content and getting rid of useless words while proofing requires looking at grammar, typos, and spelling mistakes.

Can you use the Spelling, Grammar, Cut, Copy, Paste, and Word Count tools in Microsoft Word?
- ☐ 1. I know what they are but sometimes struggle with using them.
- ☐ 2. I'm familiar with all of them except Word Count.
- ☐ 3. Yes, I'm proficient with all of these tools.

Could you create a professional-looking resume in a Word document that can be sent by email?
- ☐ 1. I wouldn't know where to begin.
- ☐ 2. It would look simple, but could definitely be sent by email.
- ☐ 3. Yes, that is how I created my current resume.

Can you use the Tracking, Bullets/Numbering, Find/Replace, Header/Footer tools in Microsoft Word?

☐ 1. I'm not sure what all of those are.
☐ 2. I know how to use some of them, but not all.
☐ 3. Yes, I am proficient with all of these tools as well as Insert Table, Borders and Shading.

Have you ever used GoogleDoc as an Online storage facility?

☐ 1. Never.
☐ 2. I've used GoogleDocs that other people have sent me.
☐ 3. I use GoogleDocs on a regular basis for work and can set it up for a group.

Do you keep an organized inbox and reply to emails in a timely manner?

☐ 1. Sometimes I read emails, but forget to reply.
☐ 2. I make sure to delete all emails that I've read or replied to and sometimes I forget to send an email.
☐ 3. I have different folders set up to organize my inbox and I always reply to emails as soon as I get them.

You are setting up your social network site. You are most likely to:

☐ 1. Post about your job on an Online thread or discussion group.
☐ 2. Stick to a professional LinkedIn profile.
☐ 3. Set the appropriate privacy settings on any Facebook and Twitter accounts you may have.

WHAT'S YOUR SKILLS WIN! SCORE?

Add the numbers you marked. See the table below to determine the number of stars.

.5	1	1.5	2	2.5	3	3.5	4	4.5	5
12-14	15-17	18-20	21-23	24-26	27-28	29-30	31-32	33-34	32-36
⭑	★	★⭑	★★	★★⭑	★★	★★⭑	★★	★★★⭑	★★★
				⭑	★	★⭑	★★	★⭑	★★

Record your initial SkillsWin! assessment score here:

_____

It is recommended that you return and take the assessment every three months. Space is provided below for you to record your SkillsWin! assessment scores.

DATE   **SCORE**

_____   _____

_____   _____

_____   _____

_____   _____

SKILL #12
WRITE WELL

Writing well means using text to effectively communicate and convey one's ideas, knowledge, and opinions.

Writing in the work world usually comes from a boss who needs a report written to inform others. It almost always takes the form of a memo ranging from a paragraph to no more than two pages and frequently requires the use of numbered points. Writing for your job will not be like writing for courses, in which the assignment is designed to help you learn something. Instead, the purpose of work writing is generally to brief others about a problem or situation and to possibly propose solutions.

BE A WINNER!

I had a freshman student who could write quickly and well. During the summer she volunteered for a Congressional candidate. One day, she found a press release put out by the campaign, revised it and showed it to the candidate. The candidate put her in charge of all press releases and paid her for the summer. This rising sophomore was asked to take a semester off to be paid as deputy campaign manager. Following that she had offers to manage other campaigns and work as a consultant. All of this from writing well. She had skills her boss needed, and there was no stopping her.

A senior human resources director at a major company says, "Being able to write clearly is a must at my company. We have a database that holds problems and potential solutions—entered by every employee in our implementation field. Our production team uses this database in order to fix problems that the rest of the company encounters. If they can't comprehend what the employee is trying to say, they can't fix it. We also collect writing samples from our potential employees. We ask a number of questions and ask them to respond—quite simple, but we can tell who can write and who cannot."

As one moves up the ladder, writing becomes even more important. If you have an idea that you can only explain verbally, you are limited to influencing only those you speak with personally. However, a one-page memo circulating throughout the organization can become part of a process that may eventually lead to the improvement and implementation of your idea. Putting your idea on paper makes it much harder for others to steal it.

THINK ABOUT IT

How well do you write? Circle your score.

1　　　**2**　　　**3**　　　**4**　　　**5**

POOR　　　　　　　　　　　　　　　OUTSTANDING

Comment on why you gave yourself this score here:

_____

_____

_____

_____

GAME CHANGERS

1 Attend a writing workshop run by your school.

2 Read one news article each day. Reading proper sentence structures will help improve your writing.

3 When someone edits your paper, record and think about their changes so you learn for the future.

MAKE A SKILL IMPROVEMENT PLAN

Describe and give examples of how you plan to improve or maintain your writing.

_____

_____

_____

_____

_____

_____

_____

SKILL #13
EDIT AND PROOF

Editing and proofing well means reviewing and correcting mistakes in written drafts.

Editing refers to organizing content between and within paragraphs, choosing the right words, and making sure the text is understandable and interesting. Proofreading is the last stage of the revision process, checking for misspellings, omissions, and grammatical mistakes. You should proofread your final draft before you submit it to anyone. Some of the proofing process is simply mechanical and is greatly helped by spell-check and grammar-checking features in Microsoft Word. The editing part, however, is more complicated, and requires as much practice and skill as writing.

Most college students consider themselves lucky if they have time to run the spell-check before they grab their papers out of the printer so they can hand them in on time. If this sounds like you, you need to know that the most critical step in learning to edit and proof is to reserve time to edit and proof. This means planning to finish what you consider to be a final draft of your paper well enough in advance of the deadline in order to carefully edit and proof it. A misspelling would only cost you a couple of points on your paper in a course, but it could spell doom in the workplace. As a senior executive says, "Who wants to buy our multi-million dollar product when we can't even spell it right? Attention to detail is key in the workforce—without it, don't bother."

Sound harsh? To put the importance of editing and proofing in proper perspective, leaving a "not" out of a business proposal is about the same as a surgeon taking out your left kidney when your right one is diseased. On the upside, if your boss knows she can throw a rough draft at you and you can edit and proof it so it is more readable, you will save her time and anguish. As long as you also excel in other areas, superiors consider editing and proofing a direct path to higher-level positions.

BE A WINNER!

Were you a person who put off starting written assignments until the last minute and had no time to edit and proof your work before handing it in? If so, you better get out of that very bad habit now. It will not be easy, since you were most likely trained not to edit and proof throughout most of your formal education, but not doing so could affect your chances of getting a job.

THINK ABOUT IT

How well do you edit and proof? Circle your score.

1   **2**   **3**   **4**   **5**

POOR   OUTSTANDING

Comment on why you gave yourself this score here:

_____

_____

_____

_____

GAME CHANGERS

1 Volunteer to proofread a friend's paper.

2 Write or edit for a school or group publication.

3 Read *The Elements of Style* by William Strunk Jr. and E.B. White and follow its rules.

MAKE A SKILL IMPROVEMENT PLAN

Describe and give examples of how you plan to improve or maintain your ability to edit and proof.

_____

_____

_____

_____

_____

_____

SKILL #14
USE WORD PROCESSING TOOLS

Using word processing tools means operating basic word processing programs and understanding how their features work for different types of products.

Whether you are using Microsoft Word, Apple Pages, or GoogleDocs, you have access to powerful tools to avoid spelling and grammar mistakes. Take time to learn how they all work because they all can increase both the efficiency and quality of your work. Ask friends who have a solid knowledge of these tools for help. Check out the menus and toolbar options.

Your ability to use these word processing tools effortlessly and effectively will impress your supervisors, especially those who may not have kept up with the latest innovations. Conversely, if you are not familiar with the time-saving and quality-increasing features of Word, you could be in deep trouble, especially if your colleague, or—even worse—your boss, is watching over your shoulder as you try to figure out the Find and Replace function five minutes before a report is due.

While I strongly recommend the use of these tools, do not assume they or your applications are always correct. You still need to edit and proof on hard copy (not on the computer screen) before you send out whatever you write.

BE A WINNER!

Every semester, several students leave a page out of their paper or have the fourth page in front of the third page. After they lose maybe as much as a quarter of the grade for that paper, they come to me and say "it looked alright on the computer screen" which means they never read a printed version. Imagine doing that in a job, where maybe you left out the page with the list of specific items charged in a bill!

THINK ABOUT IT

How well do you use word processing tools? Circle your score.

1   **2**   **3**   **4**   **5**

POOR   OUTSTANDING

Comment on why you gave yourself this score here:

_____

_____

_____

_____

GAME CHANGERS

1 Take a Microsoft Word tutorial on the official Microsoft website.

2 Take an hour to check out Word's toolbar options and consult Microsoft Help.

3 Have a friend or teacher coach you on unfamiliar Microsoft Word features, like Tracking.

MAKE A SKILL IMPROVEMENT PLAN

Describe and give examples of how you plan to improve or maintain how well you use word processing tools.

_____

_____

_____

_____

_____

_____

SKILL #15
MASTER ONLINE COMMUNICATION

Mastering online communication means using email and other electronic-based mediums to send and receive messages with proper etiquette.

Electronic communications are now used to create virtual jobs and to hold virtual meetings. Workers who travel or work from home take directions from bosses, exchange views with colleagues, and complete tasks over email. Programs like GoogleDocs are used to create an electronic, document-based forum for teamwork so that a virtual office of people anywhere in the world can exchange views. The use of chat services and webinars where a telephone conversation is facilitated by shared displays or documents is also increasing.

Communicating electronically can have its downsides also. E-mail can be a constant interuption whether you work at a desk or use a portable device, and several of these small distractions throughout the day can be a major roadblock to your success, especially if you are trying to write something. If you have become addicted to "checking" for messages from email or Twitter, you might be "caught" at a meeting and chastised. Bosses don't like to see this addiction, even if they are addicted themselves. Learn to break the habit by turning off your portable device and fixing your desktop to not alert you to incoming email messages.

Even a more serious downside is that emails can be accessed by your boss and the government forever, so be careful what you write. Loose talk in a professional setting is bad enough, but loose emailing or use of social meeting can be deadly.

BE A WINNER

One of the most important features of emailing is the ability to copy others. Three people can share comments in a series of exchange. Just hit "reply all." But like any other tool, the copy process can cause harm if you forgot who was being copied.

THINK ABOUT IT

How well do you communicate online? Circle your score.

1 **2** **3** **4** **5**

POOR   OUTSTANDING

Comment on why you gave yourself this score here:

_____

_____

_____

_____

GAME CHANGERS

1 Practice using Microsoft Outlook Express.

2 Become familiar with GoogleDocs. Use it as a way to collaborate on your next group project.

3 Have someone review the next few emails you send.

MAKE A SKILL IMPROVEMENT PLAN

Describe and give examples of how you plan to improve or maintain your ability to communicate online.

_____

_____

_____

_____

_____

_____

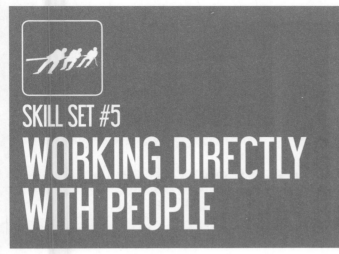

SKILL SET #5
WORKING DIRECTLY WITH PEOPLE

Knowing how to work with others is critical to your career success and also makes life a lot more pleasant. Many human resource directors, employers, and experts rate people skills as the most important of the ten Skill Sets. Because people skills are so important, they constitute two different Skill Sets in this playbook—working directly with people, which is this chapter's topic, and influencing people, which we will look at in Skill Set 6. While there is a fine line between "working with" and "influencing," these skills are different enough to warrant separate chapters. By creating these two Skill Sets, we give double weight to people skills in our list of 10 Skill Sets.

No matter where you are employed, you will find that all employers place heavy emphasis on their employees' ability to work well with others and to influence others, both within and outside of the organization. Teamwork has the potential to make or break a company or organization. Whether or not you are able to collaborate with your coworkers will make or break your future at your job. Working in teams requires you to build relationships with your team members so that you can work together more

RUNDOWN >>
Working directly with people consists of three skills:

#16 BUILDING GOOD RELATIONSHIPS
means forming and maintaining positive relations with others.

#17 WORKING IN TEAMS
means working with others to successfully complete specific tasks.

#18 TEACH OTHERS
means helping others acquire specific skills and knowledge.

effectively later. It can allow you to teach other members skills or processes specific to the job so that the entire team can be successful. You will find it much easier to gain influence within your company if you can demonstrate to your boss that you are a team player who works well with others.

SKILLS WIN! ASSESSMENT

Take the following assessment for Skill Set #5. Put a check in the box next to each question. Make sure you answer the questions honestly. If you lie, you are lying to yourself and probably will not succeed as you would like.

If you have a conflict with someone, how will you handle it?
- ☐ 1. Avoid it until it gets too important and then take an aggressive stance.
- ☐ 2. Indirectly hint that there is a problem.
- ☐ 3. Bring it up as early as possible in a non-threatening way.

If you meet someone for the first time, what would you do?
- ☐ 1. Make sure that I left a good impression.
- ☐ 2. Talk a lot to show them that I am friendly.
- ☐ 3. Show that I am interested in them by asking questions about them and showing a genuine interest.

You recently helped organize a fundraiser and want to thank those that attended, how would you thank them?
- ☐ 1. Make a general announcement during the fundraiser giving everyone a general "thank you".
- ☐ 2. Forward all supporters a mass "thank you" email.
- ☐ 3. Mail a "thank you" card to all supporters with personalized notes written to larger contributors.

You are leading a team at work to complete a project, how would you distribute tasks?
- ☐ 1. I would do most of the project on my own to make sure it was done well.
- ☐ 2. Assign each team member a task to complete.
- ☐ 3. Ask each team member to choose a specific task to complete depending on their strengths.

If you were on a team how would you make sure everyone is completing their tasks on time?
- ☐ 1. I would just have faith they'd get it done on time.
- ☐ 2. I would suggest a system to send out email reminders to every team member telling them what they should have completed.
- ☐ 3. I would suggest a system that sends reminders and requires emails indicating what tasks are completed.

When working on a team are you patient and positive?
- ☐ 1. I tend to get frustrated easily.
- ☐ 2. I try to stay positive, but sometimes I get annoyed with other group members.
- ☐ 3. Being positive and patient is the best way to keep the team focused and motivated.

Do you have experience as a mentor or coach?
- ☐ 1. No.
- ☐ 2. I was a mentor in high school, but haven't done anything since.
- ☐ 3. Yes, I am currently a coach for a little league baseball team.

Do you consciously think about being a good role model to those around you?
- ☐ 1. Never.
- ☐ 2. Depends on what mood I am in.
- ☐ 3. I always strive to be a good role model in everything I do.

Have you ever motivated your colleagues in a learning experience?
- ☐ 2. Never.
- ☐ 2. I've had some success but it came with a lot of difficulty.
- ☐ 3. I usually get people to do what I want them to do.

WHAT'S YOUR SKILLS WIN! SCORE?

Add the numbers you marked. See the table below to determine the number of stars.

.5	1	1.5	2	2.5	3	3.5	4	4.5	5
12-14	15-17	18-20	21-23	24-26	27-28	29-30	31-32	33-34	32-36

Record your initial SkillsWin! assessment score here:

_____

It is recommended that you return and take the assessment every three months. Space is provided below for you to record your SkillsWin! assessment scores.

DATE   SCORE

_____   _____

_____   _____

_____   _____

_____   _____

SKILL #16
BUILD GOOD RELATIONSHIPS

Building good relationships means forming and maintaining positive relations with others.

Building good relationships with others is no easy task because it takes time and constant attention. Doing this well requires attention to a broad array of factors, including different cultural, ethnic, social, and economic backgrounds. Being sensitive and understanding these factors can often prevent struggles over power and authority or conflicts over competing interests, which sometimes irreparably damage relationships. Given these factors, it's important to practice establishing good working relationships in all settings.

One of the first tests of your ability to build a good relationship comes when you are interviewed for a job. Establishing a good relationship with your interviewer will determine whether or not you get the job.

BE A WINNER!

The quickest and most powerful way to improve your relationships with people is to practice Dale Carnegie's principles. Carnegie's book *How to Win Friends and Influence* has been published in 55 languages and has remained top seller since it was first published in 1936. Like this playbook, you can't just read Carnegie's principles. You have to practice them everyday so that they become habit and a way of life.

Once you get the job, your success will depend on developing good working relationships with people throughout the organization. Good working relationships make it possible to work more efficiently and effectively, not to mention more pleasantly. People with whom you have good relationships can also help you learn about or even obtain jobs throughout your career—this is usually called networking. Whether or not you have people who are willing to help you is a direct result of your ability (or inability) to establish good relationships. For example, if you've developed a good working relationship with your boss, you might open unexpected possibilities for your future. One of the surest paths to career advancement is when your boss moves to another company and hires you six months later because he or she thinks you have done a great job and trusts you.

THINK ABOUT IT

How well do you form relationships with others? Circle your score.

1   2   3   4   5

POOR   OUTSTANDING

Comment on why you gave yourself this score here:

_____

_____

_____

_____

GAME CHANGERS

1 Make a conscious effort to think before you speak. Be careful not to offend others. If you aren't sure, it's best to keep quiet.

2 Always give people your full attention during a conversation. Listen, make eye contact and stay off your cell phone.

3 If you must criticize someone, start and end with a genuine compliment. People will be more receptive and less likely to take your comments personally.

MAKE A SKILL IMPROVEMENT PLAN

Describe and give examples of how you plan to improve or maintain your ability to build relationships with others.

_____

_____

_____

_____

_____

_____

WORK IN TEAMS

Working in teams means working with others to successfully complete specific tasks.

Most people initially do not like working in teams. This is natural since we live in a society that praises individualism and competition. If you are very competitive, you do not want to depend on others, you want the control. If you are relaxed, you do not want the hyper people on the team bugging you.

However, to be successful, you need to learn to like, or at least tolerate teamwork. Many businesses set up virtual teams in which the team members rarely meet face to face, if at all but work through the Internet and phone. There are also specific skills required for working in a team, including being able to reach agreements with others, understanding the importance of concurring on how decisions will be made, running productive meetings, and designating roles within the team.

BE A WINNER!

You have probably held the statement, "there is no I in team." This is misleading because each individual in a team must take responsibility to make the team as strong as possible. Sometimes this means compromising, but sometimes it means remaining true to yourself. The best teams integrate individual creativity with a common commitment to the mission.

Perhaps the most important traits you need for teamwork is patience and tolerance for the process. Teams rarely perform as well as team members think they should perform. Learning to be tolerant and to carefully pick your battles is essential to being a good team member.

Failure to work well in teams in the workplace leads to poor job reviews. Conversely, working well in teams gains you positive points throughout the organization and may even lead to promotions. You can whine about your team to your significant other, but always be positive about your team when you are at work in word and deed. It's frustrating, but good teamwork is the law of most high-functioning organizations.

THINK ABOUT IT

How well do you work in teams? Circle your score.

1   **2**   **3**   **4**   **5**

POOR   OUTSTANDING

Comment on why you gave yourself this score here:

_____

_____

_____

_____

GAME CHANGERS

1 Learn each of your team member's names by the second meeting.

2 Divide up work according to to each team member's strengths.

3 Practice being patient with your team members.

MAKE A SKILL IMPROVEMENT PLAN

Describe and give examples of how you plan to improve or maintain your ability to work in teams.

_____

_____

_____

_____

_____

_____

SKILL #18
TEACH OTHERS

Teaching others means helping others acquire specific skills and knowledge.

Teaching is a process in which one person—the teacher—takes action to improve what another person—the learner—knows or does. Within that definition, knowing how to teach is essential in every aspect of your life, whether it be teaching your little brother how to get dates or teaching your roommate to stop throwing trash on your side of the room. You may even find yourself needing to teach others in a formal job setting, maybe by teaching a new employee how to work the fax machine or explaining the details of your company's budget process.

The skills of a good teacher grow out of many of the skills discussed in this book. Verbal communication is critical but so is asking and answering the right questions. Beyond that, teaching requires a consciousness about where the learner is, and the ability to implement strategies that get the learner to move to where they want to be. The best companies are committed to encouraging or even requiring senior staff to guide and educate junior staff. You will need to become a teacher within your organization soon after you arrive, and your capacity to "train" others to do your job will also help you move into other positions. Sometimes the word "mentor" or "coach" is used, but it still means teaching—and mostly teaching by example. The teaching and mentoring ability of an employee usually leads to higher management positions and raises for that person.

BE A WINNER!

You will have no choice but to be a teacher in your professional and personal life. Everyone has the capacity to be a good teacher because it is part of the human condition. If you are aware of when and how you are teaching and reflect on how to do it best, you will be a good teacher. Remember that teaching is not telling. Be sure to show how to perform the task while also explaining it step by step.

THINK ABOUT IT

How well do you teach others? Circle your score.

1   **2**   **3**   **4**   **5**

POOR   OUTSTANDING

Comment on why you gave yourself this score here:

_____

_____

_____

_____

GAME CHANGERS

1 Tutor a friend who needs help in a class in which you excel.

2 Join a mentoring group such as Big Brothers Big Sisters.

3 Volunteer to provide an orientation to a new employee where you work.

MAKE A SKILL IMPROVEMENT PLAN

Describe and give examples of how you plan to improve or maintain your own ability to teach others.

_____

_____

_____

_____

_____

_____

SKILL SET #6
INFLUENCING PEOPLE

orking with your colleagues and others outside the organization sometimes requires you to treat them as objects of influence, in addition to maintaining good relationships with them. This may sound a little harsh, but it is reality. Keep in mind that there are many styles of managing, selling, politicking, and leading. You will need to develop the style that is both effective and comfortable for you. Practicing these skills now outside of the workplace in different settings like in groups, clubs, or at home is important, because it will give you the opportunity to find and develop your personal style through a process of trial and error.

Another theme in this chapter is the role of honesty and character in the actions you take as a manager, salesperson, politician, and leader. All of these roles require you to convince others to do something that they would not otherwise do. Deceit and the arbitrary or unjust use of power are tempting in these situations, especially if you are faced with a roadblock or see others use these methods without facing consequences. Remember that dishonesty always catches up with you eventually, which is why it is important to learn how to control that temptation as soon as possible. Doing so will serve you well both professionally and personally in the long run.

RUNDOWN >>

Influencing people consists of four skills:

#19 MANAGE EFFECTIVELY
means delegating tasks to a group of people that you are responsible for, and ensuring that those tasks are completed on time and meet defined standards.

#20 SELL SUCCESSFULLY
means convincing someone to approve an idea or buy a product.

#21 POLITICK WISELY
means gaining the support of people in power in order to accomplish a positive change or correct a negative condition.

#22 LEAD EFFECTIVELY
means gaining the support of people in power in order to accomplish a positive change or correct a negative condition.

SKILL SET #6
SKILLS WIN! ASSESSMENT

Take the following assessment for Skill Set #6. Put a check in the box next to each question. Make sure you answer the questions honestly. If you lie, remember that the only person you are lying to is yourself, and you probably will not succeed as you would like.

When you are asked to manage a group of people, you are most likely to:
- ☐ 1. Don't know because I have never managed anyone.
- ☐ 2. Usually tell them what to do because I know they will do it.
- ☐ 3. Be clear on my expectations but send reminders and check on team members occasionally.

In a management position, I like to:
- ☐ 1. See negative feedback as a threat to my authority.
- ☐ 2. Let the group decide what to do and go with their opinion even if I disagree.
- ☐ 3. Listen to suggestions from the team members but recognize that I have primary responsibility for the team's success.

I see managing a team as:
- ☐ 1. Something to be avoided at all costs.
- ☐ 2. A challenge to take up regardless of the situation.
- ☐ 3. Something to seriously consider and take up only if I think I can meet the challenge.

When you fail or get rejected from something, you are most likely to:
- ☐ 1. Stop doing it and give up.
- ☐ 2. Get discouraged but continue working.
- ☐ 3. Cope with reflection and work to improve my chances of success.

If you were to have to sell something how would you go about doing it?
- ☐ 1. Try to convince customers my product is best no matter what they say.
- ☐ 2. Sell myself first.
- ☐ 3. Start with learning about the customers' needs and shape my presentation based on that.

How good are you at selling stuff? How often do you need motivation to help you continue your work?
- ☐ 1. Never sold anything and don't ever want to.
- ☐ 2. I can convince my friends and family to buy stuff but don't have much luck with strangers.
- ☐ 3. I realize that many times I will need to sell something no matter what career I am in and try whenever I can.

Can you identify the people you need on your side to get the decision (like your promotion) you want?
- ☐ 1. I usually think that if I have a good idea, most people will be on my side.
- ☐ 2. I will try to figure out who is on my side and who is not, based on what I know.
- ☐ 3. Spend time gathering information about the views and power of everyone who might influence the decision.

If you had an idea how would you decrease opposition to the idea?
- ☐ 1. If it's a good idea then there will be no opposition.
- ☐ 2. I can see how some people would be opposed to it, but I don't know how to make them change their positions to support it.
- ☐ 3. I would determine why they are opposed and will make adjustments to answer their concerns.

If you have a list of those who support and opposed you on a decision you would:
- ☐ 1. Assume everyone is equally important.
- ☐ 2. Work on those who have the most power.
- ☐ 3. Try to build support among all players and focus most on those who are most powerful.

What is the key to successful leadership?
- ☐ 1. Having a good idea.
- ☐ 2. Having a good relationship with people you wish to lead.
- ☐ 3. Being able to inspire people to work for an agreed upon goal.

Do you have any leadership experience?
- ☐ 1. I tend to follow rather than lead.
- ☐ 2. I have taken the lead on a few projects, but they always stress me out.
- ☐ 3. Yes, I am often assigned or take on leadership positions.

The best way to lead is to:
- ☐ 1. Be in front of the group to show the way.
- ☐ 2. Be like a shepherd and lead from behind.
- ☐ 3. There is no best way.

WHAT'S YOUR SKILLS WIN! SCORE?

Add the numbers you marked. See the table below to determine the number of stars.

.5	1	1.5	2	2.5	3	3.5	4	4.5	5
12-14	15-17	18-20	21-23	24-26	27-28	29-30	31-32	33-34	32-36
✴	★	★✴	★★	★★ ✴	★★ ★	★★ ★✴	★★ ★★	★★★ ★✴	★★★ ★★

Record your initial SkillsWin! score here:

_____

It is recommended that you return and take the assessment every three months. Space is provided below for you to record your SkillsWin! assessment score.

DATE   **SCORE**

_____   _____

_____   _____

_____   _____

_____   _____

SKILL #19
MANAGE EFFECTIVELY

Managing Effectively means delegating tasks to a group of people that you are responsible for, and ensuring that those tasks are completed on time and meet defined standards.

When you manage others, your task is to convince people to do their assigned jobs competently and on time. In other words, managing people is using the human resources assigned to you over which you have some influence, but little control. For this reason, management is always stressful, and effective managers are in short supply.

Effective managers usually come up through the ranks. They have performed well in their entry-level jobs and convinced those who managed them that they would be able to manage their former peers. To get the most from their people, managers need to build on many of the skills already discussed, especially those described in chapter five. They must also know how to use the tools their organization gives them, including salaries, benefits, and training programs, to motivate those they manage.

Good managers have to maintain the respect of those they manage by encouraging them and listening to their feedback.

Management potential is a key consideration, especially in higher paying entry-level jobs, and it may be part of the interviewer's agenda when meeting with you as a prospective employee. In order for organizations to grow, they need to recruit people who can eventually take over the jobs of the top leaders, thus allowing the top leaders to move on to new fields. These leaders want you to do your job in a way that makes their task as your manager less burdensome.

BE A WINNER!

You can demonstrate your ability to manage effectively no matter where you work. Think that your job in retail or food service could never amount to more than a dead-end job? Remember that every manager has to start somewhere. A 19-year-old was in community college and also a manager at a local McDonalds. She obtained the manager position because she showed her boss at the McDonalds that she could manage people. After a couple of years, the owner of 40 franchises offered her a job in the corporate offices with a salary of $60,000 per year. Not bad for a 21 year-old.

THINK ABOUT IT

How well do you manage effectively? Circle your score.

1   **2**   **3**   **4**   **5**

POOR   OUTSTANDING

Comment on why you gave yourself this score here:

_____

_____

_____

_____

GAME CHANGERS

1 Lead a fundraising event at your school so you can practice managing individuals.

2 Remember to delegate work equally and do your best not to play favorites when you are in a management position.

3 Know with whom you are working so you can use individuals skills to your groups advantage.

MAKE A SKILL IMPROVEMENT PLAN

Describe and give clear examples of how you plan to improve or maintain how well you manage others.

_____

_____

_____

_____

_____

_____

SKILL #20
SELL SUCCESSFULLY

Selling successfully means convincing someone to approve an idea or buy a product.

You probably think selling is about selling jeans at the Gap, or about cold calling to peddle charities, politicians, or products and services from kitchen knives to insurance. Selling successfully usually involves a higher skill level that extends beyond what is necessary at these sorts of jobs.

The traits of a good salesperson depend on almost every single Skill Sroup mentioned in this book. You have to work hard, stay healthy, have excellent communication and people skills, and be good at problem solving and analyzing information. Several characteristics critical to being an effective salesperson are being able to handle sustained and continuous rejection, keeping pressure on yourself to work hard, and having solid product knowledge.

Get rid of negative thoughts about sales before you enter the workforce. Those who make it to the top of every field are always good at selling themselves, their products, and their ideas. Sales skills can lead to very large incomes and high corporate positions because the number of people who can be successful are in very short supply. Also remember that:

- Selling is a very good training ground for all other professions because it involves synthesizing information and persuading people.

- If you are a successful salesperson you will have lots of free time and excellent contacts to be a mover and a shaker by the time you are 40.

Even if you have no interest in a sales job, taking the time to develop your sales tools is a worthwhile investment that will be handy during your job interviews and in every job you take.

DID YOU KNOW

Regardless of which career you pursue, you will ultimately need to be a salesperson. The most successful lawyers are those who bring in new clients. The most successful government workers are those who sell themselves and their departments to others. Even teaching incorporates a sales component– selling your students on the importance of a subject may be more critical than giving good lectures. And, if you want to make the world better, you will be selling "change" to others.

THINK ABOUT IT

How well do you sell successfully? Circle your score.

1 **2** **3** **4** **5**

POOR   OUTSTANDING

Comment on why you gave yourself this score here:

_____

_____

_____

_____

GAME CHANGERS

1 Approach people and ask them to contribute to your favorite charity.

2 Identify someone who is successful in selling their ideas. Take note of how they are able to convince people about their ideas.

3 Brainstorm how you could advance in your school or your job by selling yourself and your ideas.

MAKE A SKILL IMPROVEMENT PLAN

Describe and give clear examples of how you plan to improve or maintain how well you sell successfully.

_____

_____

_____

_____

_____

_____

SKILL #21
POLITICK WISELY

Politik wisely means gaining the support of people in power in order to accomplish a positive change or correct a negative condition.

You will find that playing politics is the price of career success, especially as you move up the career ladder. If you don't want to be political, don't complain about those who are. Playing office politics requires understanding the role of power, authority, and self-interest. In short, the reality is that people, not reason, control decisions, and politics is the art of getting people on your side.

Wherever you work, you will face a long history of relationships and power structures. The easiest and perhaps least risky path to follow is to do what you are told and refrain from calling for substantial change, especially the first day or even year.

Playing politics well requires that you avoid whining and complaining in the workplace. If you need to vent, wait until you get off work. Don't complain to your colleagues, and never go over the head of your immediate supervisor unless you are prepared for the worst. Instead, realize that the political forces within the organization are generally averse to change and recognize that you must always be planning as though it were a political campaign. Good politicians in any organization build coalitions to support their ideas.

From this discussion, it should be clear that developing strategies and techniques to convince your superiors to make the decisions you want—whether it's giving you a bigger salary or altering an existing policy—are skills necessary for your career. From the day you start work, you will see and hear things that will push you to react, languishing in a dead-end position. The most important path to follow is to look for compromises in most situations. This way you will not create any permanent enemies.

BE A WINNER!

Don't be like a student of mine who was suggesting additional projects he could do to his supervisor as an intern. The supervisor called me and said she was planning to fire him because he appeared to not be interested in what he was hired to do. I gave him a heads-up to keep his mouth shut and just do what he was asked. He stayed on and actually got most of the opportunities he was looking for without asking.

THINK ABOUT IT

How well do you politik wisely? Circle your score.

1   **2**   **3**   **4**   **5**

POOR   OUTSTANDING

Comment on why you gave yourself this score here:

_____

_____

_____

_____

GAME CHANGERS

1 Make a list of people who support and oppose an idea you create. Figure out how you could convince some to change their minds.

2 Participate in an organization and work to implement action.

3 Work to join groups that make decisions and try to become actively involved within the group.

MAKE A SKILL IMPROVEMENT PLAN

Describe and give clear examples of how you plan to improve or maintain how well you politik wisely.

_____

_____

_____

_____

_____

_____

THINK ABOUT IT

How well do you lead effectively? Circle your score.

1   **2**   **3**   **4**   **5**

POOR   OUTSTANDING

Comment on why you gave yourself this score here:

_____

_____

_____

_____

GAME CHANGERS

1 Not sure how to begin leading others? Try starting your own new organization.

2 Observe a leader whom you respect and try to use their techniques.

3 Be open and willing to listen to suggestions from the people you work with. They will respect you more as a leader if they feel you're willing to listen.

MAKE A SKILL IMPROVEMENT PLAN

Describe and give clear examples of how you plan to improve or maintain how well you effictively lead.

_____

_____

_____

_____

_____

_____

SKILL SET #7
GATHERING INFORMATION

Knowing how to collect information is critical to any job. You cannot perform your job without having the necessary information. Getting information is more than a high speed scavenger hunt. It requires focus in the face of chaos. Not being sure what you are looking for creates substantial difficulties. Frequently, people requesting the information are not clear. Even if they are, the first piece you bring them may be a surprise and the information request changes.

People usually refer to seeking information as peeling away layers of an onion. You start with basic information to understand the questions you want answered, and then you

RUNDOWN >>

Gathering information consists of six skills:

#23 SEARCH THE WEB
means using the Internet to obtain relevant information quickly and efficiently.

#24 USE LIBRARY HOLDINGS
means searching through archives, databases, and records for information on a topic relevant to an area of research or interest.

#25 USE COMMERCIAL DATABASES
means searching through archives, databases, and records for information on a topic relevant to an area of research or interest.

#26 CONDUCT INTERVIEWS
means asking another person questions in order to obtain information you need.

#27 USE SURVEYS
means administering and analyzing surveys to collect data for a specific purpose.

#28 KEEP AND USE RECORDS
means creating, maintaining and using records such as financial records (budget), personal records (birth certificate), and legal records (settlements).

need to find more information to answer the questions, which leads to more questions and more information. As you analyze your information, you will need to ask better questions. Sometimes you realize that your information base is weak and that you need to search for more specific information. Collecting information is an unlimited, open-ended process, but we have to start somewhere. This chapter features six skills that will provide you with the know-how to collect different kinds of information essential to most jobs.

SKILL SET #7
SKILLS WIN! ASSESSMENT

Take the following assessment for Skill Set #7. Put a check in the box next to each question. Make sure you answer the questions honestly. If you lie, you are lying to yourself and probably will not succeed as you would like.

Where would you start to look for job/internship opportunities on the Internet?
☐ 1. I would type "job opps" into Google.
☐ 2. I would try Monster or Monster College.
☐ 3. I would use multiple search engines like Google, Monster, and O-net.

If you had to find demographic information about your hometown, you would:
☐ 1. Use Wikipedia.
☐ 2. Google your town and use what information comes up.
☐ 3. Look up your towns official webpage, as well as other sources like the national census to compare information to compile the most accurate results.

You are searching for a healthy recipe for dinner. You are most likely to:
☐ 1. Type "Find a healthy recipe" into a search bar, click on the first link you find.
☐ 2. Go to the official website of your favorite chef for healthy recipes.
☐ 3. Search for a positive reviewed website with healthy options with the calorie content.

If you needed to find a book on a specific topic and are in a library, how would you go about your search?
☐ 1. Wander around the library in hopes of something catching your eye.
☐ 2. Ask the librarian to find books that would apply.
☐ 3. Use the library catalogue and database to search for books on the topic and ask a librarian if you need help locating something.

You want to look up a newspaper from November 1950, how would you go about doing so using library resources?
☐ 1. I have no idea.
☐ 2. Ask the library for help.
☐ 3. Use the library catalogue and database system to look through there newspaper records and ask a librarian if I needed help.

Have you ever used a commercial database to find information?
☐ 1. Never.
☐ 2. I know of a few but don't know how to use them well.
☐ 3. Yes, I often use ProQuest Direct and other databases.

If you wanted information about a topic from a variety of sources how would you find it?
☐ 1. Google the topic and use the Online articles in Online publications.
☐ 2. Individually search for your topic for each different source (magazine, newspapers, books).
☐ 3. Use a database to look up your topic, which will give you results in a variety of sources.

You have been searching background on a topic for a few minutes and are having a hard time finding any information. You are most likely to:
☐ 1. Give up and begin to look at some of the links that do come up.
☐ 2. Keep paging through the search results.
☐ 3. Try searching different yet related terms.

Do you have experience conducting interviews?
☐ 1. No.
☐ 2. I've had a lot of interviews to reflect on how to do one.
☐ 3. Yes, I have conducted interviews multiple times.

How do you create questions for your interviews?
- ☐ 1. Wing it and think of some questions on the spot.
- ☐ 2. Ask about the interviewee's background and then see where it goes from there.
- ☐ 3. Find out about their background and then ask about specific scenarios they might encounter on the job.

When the interviewee is done answering a question, you are most likely to:
- ☐ 1. Ask them about an unrelated topic.
- ☐ 2. Go directly on the next question.
- ☐ 3. Ask a follow-up question to clarify anything that was said.

You are trying to survey people about their opinions of the current town council. You are most likely to:
- ☐ 1. Ask your friends and family their opinions on the members.
- ☐ 2. Ask every employee of your town's local government about their opinions on the council members.
- ☐ 3. Call every fifth number in the phone book about their opinions on the town council.

Have you ever created and conducted a survey?
- ☐ 1. Never.
- ☐ 2. I've conducted one, but never created my own.
- ☐ 3. Yes, and analyzed the data.

After collecting open ended survey data for a project you are most likely to:
- ☐ 1. Ready every response and try to remember the consensus for each question.
- ☐ 2. Write down every response for each question on the survey and then analyze the data.
- ☐ 3. Group the answers together in similar categories and analyze the data from there.

Do you keep track of what you have accomplished in a given day?
- ☐ 1. Not really.
- ☐ 2. I keep track of it in my head.
- ☐ 3. Yes, I keep a checklist of everything I've completed throughout the day.

You receive countless emails every day, and feel a little overwhelmed with the disorganization of your inbox. You are most likely to:
- ☐ 1. Continue to just let all emails sit in your general inbox.
- ☐ 2. Delete the majority of the emails , you think a fresh start will be best.
- ☐ 3. Begin to create specific folders to group like emails within your inbox.

WHAT'S YOUR SKILLS WIN! SCORE?

Add the numbers you marked. See the table below to determine the number of stars.

.5	1	1.5	2	2.5	3	3.5	4	4.5	5
18-21	22-25	26-29	30-33	34-37	38-41	42-45	46-49	50-52	53-54
✯	★	★✯	★★	★★	★★	★★	★★	★★★	★★★
				✯	★	★✯	★★	★✯	★★

Record your initial SkillsWin! score here: _____

It is recommended that you return and take the assessment every three months. Space is provided below for you to record your SkillsWin! assessment score.

DATE	**SCORE**
_____	_____
_____	_____
_____	_____

SKILL #23
SEARCHING THE WEB

Searching the Web means using the Internet to obtain relevant information quickly and efficiently.

Finding information on the Internet may seem easy, but finding the information you need and can trust on the Internet is much harder. Internet research can be risky and lead to poor results unless you have solid grasp of web research (as well as many of the 10 Skill Sets). The key is to assess the authors and publication sources that provide the information. Learn about the strengths and weaknesses of various search engines and how to use them so you can learn more about the organization or people who have published the information you found. Are they reliable? Would others in your profession consider this website a good source of relevant professional information? Use your web-search and critical thinking skills to avoid giving your boss information that is incomplete or incorrect.

You can also find sites on the Web that will do things for you. For example, some sites can produce correct citations for different citation styles. Professors in different discipline use different citation systems. There are sites that allow you to tabulate survey results or translate reports written in other languages into English.

The Internet is an essential tool for exploring careers, finding out about companies, and most important, getting jobs.

BE A WINNER!

Wikipedia was heavily criticized in its early years because anyone was able edit its content. However, Wikipedia's collaborative editing policies encourage ongoing improvement of its articles. Moreover, articles contain clinks to other reliable published links. Wikipedia is a great place to get an initial factual briefing for some kinds of background factors.

THINK ABOUT IT

How well do you search the Web? Circle your score.

1   **2**   **3**   **4**   **5**

POOR   OUTSTANDING

Comment on why you gave yourself this score here:

_____

_____

_____

_____

GAME CHANGERS

1 Google a friend's name and try to find any articles, stories, or publications that are actually about that person, not just someone else with their name.

2 Use Wikipedia to learn about a historical figure and study how information is presented and documented.

3 Become familiar with U.S. Census Data by looking up your town and state at census.gov.

MAKE A SKILL IMPROVEMENT PLAN

Describe and give clear examples of how you plan to improve or maintain how well you search the Web.

_____

_____

_____

_____

_____

_____

SKILL #24
USE LIBRARY HOLDINGS

Using library holdings means searching through archives, databases, and records for information on a topic relevant to an area of research or interest.

The library used to be a place where you found collections of printed information. Today a library is a more complex system that houses some printed information, but also provides electronic access to an almost unlimited amount of publications and multimedia formats. You need to know how to locate information in a large library by using that library's website and Online catalog, as well as its hard copy and electronic publications.

Your job may not require going to a large library, but it will require you to search for information. In addition, you may find yourself required to use the holdings of a corporate or other private archive to locate information, or perhaps even consult a government library, including federal, state, and local records. Efficiently and effectively using library research tools and actual holdings will prepare you to use those and other tools to research relevant topics such as mailing lists, government programs, and the work of relevant professional associations for future employers.

Some libraries may give you access to commercial databases that would require large expenses for you or your employer. Moreover, today's librarians in public libraries are usually savvy about searching existing databases.

BE A WINNER

Librarians can be your friends. They may look intimidating, but when approaching them for help, you will find they will be glad to help you, especially if you ask something other than where are the restrooms. They love to solve your problems in finding things because that is what they were trained to do.

THINK ABOUT IT

How well do you use library holdings? Circle your score.

1	**2**	**3**	**4**	**5**
POOR				OUTSTANDING

Comment on why you gave yourself this score here:

_____

_____

_____

_____

GAME CHANGERS

1 Spend some time in the library learning what information is available in hard copy and electronic format.

2 Rummage around the aisles for a topic that interests you.

3 Ask your librarian questions about sources when working on a research project.

MAKE A SKILL IMPROVEMENT PLAN

Describe and give clear examples of how you plan to improve or maintain your ability to use library holdings?

_____

_____

_____

_____

_____

_____

SKILL #25
USE COMMERCIAL DATABASES

Using commercial databases means using certain Online sources beyond websites to gain reliable information.

The term "database" has two very different meanings. First, it can mean a computer software program where you or your employer record information, like Microsoft Excel or Access. A database also could mean a large set of published information available electronically. In this section, we will talk about the latter—the growing number of specialized bodies of highly organized information available in libraries and for purchase.

The explosion of information available in print and on the Web has caused people or businesses to find relevant and accurate information quickly and are willing to pay. As a result, databases charge subscription fees in exchange for continuous archiving, organization, and delivery of that information. Sources one can find in these paid databases are usually more focused and more reliable than random source information found on the Web.

One of the largest journalistic and legal database sources is LexisNexis. ProQuest also offers many database products with financial, academic, historical, and statistical information. Free government websites are usually as reliable and useful as commercial databases. In fact, many commercial databases import vast amounts of free government information. Additionally, high-quality publications in the sciences, healthcare, and medicine are increasingly offered free Online, especially when the research behind those published works is funded by the U.S. government. You need to be aware of these databases, understand how to find appropriate ones, and able to use their sophisticated search engines to conduct research.

BE A WINNER!

In the corporate world, data-mining means obtaining information about potential customers or competitors. In this case, you are the miner and the commercial databases are like gold mines; it is a much cleaner and less dangerous source of valuable nuggets.

THINK ABOUT IT

How well do you use commercial databases? Circle your score.

1   2   3   4   5

POOR   OUTSTANDING

Comment on why you gave yourself this score here:

_____

_____

_____

_____

GAME CHANGERS

1 Make a list of all the commercial databases at your school or local library.

2 Use Lexis-Nexis Academic next time you have a research project for statistical information.

3 Look up a newspaper article on ProQuest for a topic you are interested in.

MAKE A SKILL IMPROVEMENT PLAN

Describe and give clear examples of how you plan to improve your ability to use commercial databases.

_____

_____

_____

_____

_____

_____

SKILL #26
CONDUCT INTERVIEWS

Conducting interviews means asking another person questions in order to obtain information you need.

The single most important reason for conducting effective interviews is to save time and to ask more questions after you get the first answer. With little background,

BE A WINNER

You probably already know how to do this if you are like one of my former students who writes: "You can get scores of questions answered on the Internet, but you can get information you trust from actual people, and you can get it fast." For example, asking a neighbor or a friend's parents about the best place in town to buy a car is a lot easier and more dependable than searching through tons of automobile websites. To get the information you want, you need to figure out the best people and the best questions to ask so that you can get you want quickly.

you can get more basic information and leads in less time than you would by going to the library or searching databases and websites.

Even if you ask someone who knows a little information on a subject about the best book, article, website, or database, you will be way ahead of the game. If you are good at interviewing, you will be able to help your boss when he says, "Find out about X and brief me on it." This principle applies to any kind of information search. To illustrate, the most important part of a job search is finding information about companies and career opportunities.

You can start with the Web, but you are going to save time and have better results if you ask career counselors, employers at job fairs, and through "informational" interviews from people who work at the company you are investigating. After doing that, you can search for information on the Web.

THINK ABOUT IT

How well do you conduct interviews? Circle your score.

1   **2**   **3**   **4**   **5**

POOR   OUTSTANDING

Comment on why you gave yourself this score here:

_____

_____

_____

_____

GAME CHANGERS

1 Research your topics and write your questions before the interview.

2 Listen to the interviewee during the meeting (you should only be talking 10% of the time).

3 Use a recorder during the interview and summarize the notes after.

MAKE A SKILL IMPROVEMENT PLAN

Describe and give clear examples of how you plan to improve or maintain how well you conduct interviews.

_____

_____

_____

_____

_____

_____

SKILL #27
USE SURVEYS

Using surveys means administering and analyzing surveys to collect data for a specific purpose.

There are many different kinds of surveys, ranging from customer surveys and focus groups to market research and public opinion polls. You should learn the limitations of every survey and how to adjust for those limitations. Everyone who graduates from college does not need to know how to conduct a survey, but everyone needs to know how to interpret survey findings.

BE A WINNER

Lauren, one of my students, interned at a company that was about to hire a consulting firm to do a survey. She told her supervisor about SurveyMonkey and saved them $20,000. You can imagine what her supervisor thought about this intern after that! Instead of entering data in a spreadsheet all summer, she went to conferences all over the U.S. with her employer and helped administer the surveys. She was offered a guaranteed job when she graduated, even though she was a rising junior at the time.

Any job you take will be in an organization that works with a large number of people, either within the organization or as customers or both. Having information about the characteristics and attitudes of these people will be crucial, and surveys are frequently used to acquire that information. In some cases, you may even participate in designing and implementing a survey. At a bare minimum, you need to be a skeptical consumer of the surveys that come your way by asking the right questions about the quality of the sample and the biases in the surveys.

You should also be familiar with a product called SurveyMonkey (www.surveymonkey.com), which, according to their website, is used by 100 percent of the Fortune 500 companies. SurveyMonkey is a web tool that can be used free on a limited basis to conduct surveys over the Internet. SurveyMonkey collects the information and dumps it into an Excel spreadsheet so you don't even have to enter the data.

THINK ABOUT IT

How well do you use surveys? Circle your score.

1   **2**   **3**   **4**   **5**

POOR   OUTSTANDING

Comment on why you gave yourself this score here:

_____

_____

_____

_____

GAME CHANGERS

1 Create a paper survey on any topic. Ask five friends to complete it and gather the results.

2 Create a survey at SurveyMonkey.com survey to develop ideas for a project.

3 Analyze the results from a survey and explain the results to an interested group.

MAKE A SKILL IMPROVEMENT PLAN

Describe and give clear examples of how you plan to improve or maintain your ability to use surveys.

_____

_____

_____

_____

_____

_____

SKILL #28
KEEP AND USE RECORDS

Keeping and using records means creating, maintaining and using records such as financial records (budget), personal records (birth certificate), and legal records (settlements).

Record keeping may sound like the ultimate mindless activity, but, unfortunately, keeping and checking records is a critical skill. It requires organization and attention to detail. The best way to improve your record keeping is to do it for your own expenses and incomes. Even keeping the birth dates of your family in an organized place will help you improve your record keeping.

Whether you have a job in business, government, or the nonprofit sector, maintaining records of expenses and services are critical. Lawyers charge clients by fifteen-minute intervals. Keeping good records is not only for businesses in which accounting procedures are the ultimate in record keeping, but also for nonprofits that must show their funders and the Internal Revenue Service what they are doing with their money.

BE A WINNER

A successful salesman wrote a book in which he said that keeping detailed records was a key to his success. By keeping records he saw that 70 percent of his sales were made on his first call, 23 percent on his second, and only 7 percent on his third call. His conclusion was that he should make more first-time calls and fewer third-time calls. He reported that this exercise in record-keeping doubled the amount of money he earned for each phone call he made.

On a personal level, record keeping can mean money. You may need to put in requests for travel reimbursements. Develop a capacity to keep good records for what you do. More importantly, learn how to use and assess the quality of the records that are important for making decisions in your job. Just in case you are not convinced, think about what will happen to you if you don't keep receipts for your expenses when the IRS calls and tells you that will be audited.

Record keeping can take many forms. Keep physical documents in a place where you can find them easily. You can record things by hand in an orderly way and also remember where you put, for example, the checkbook. Computers can be a tremendous help in keeping record especially if there are a lot of items. Just remember what folders and drives you are saving the records to.

THINK ABOUT IT

How well do you keep and use records? Circle your score.

1　　**2**　　**3**　　**4**　　**5**

POOR　　　　　　　　　　　　OUTSTANDING

Comment on why you gave yourself this score here:

_____

_____

_____

_____

GAME CHANGERS

1 Keep all receipts and bank statements in a binder or an electronic file.

2 Become the secretary for a club or organization.

3 Volunteer to take notes in a meeting and report back to the group at the next meeting.

MAKE A SKILL IMPROVEMENT PLAN

Describe and give clear examples of how you plan to improve or maintain how well you keep and use records.

_____

_____

_____

_____

_____

_____

SKILL SET #8
USING QUANTITATIVE TOOLS

This Skill Set covers the three most basic quantitative tools you will need for your career and your personal life. Most positions will require you to use these skills, and you may even be tested for them as a part of the hiring process.

If you are not a numbers person, you'll see that anybody can achieve the skill level required. If you are a numbers person, heed this word of warning: getting 800 on your quantitative SAT, being a whiz at calculus, and knowing how to calculate the most exotic statistics are not the same as using quantitative tools. You may consider the skills covered in this set trivial, but application of simple quantifiable tools requires practice.

You probably already know how to use simple graphs like those with bars and simple tables that show how numbers are related to each other. Many people are not used to thinking with or are not good at using graphs and charts to make a point about a problem or decision that they face even though the mechanics are easy.

Whatever job you take will require you to analyze numbers and present them. Graphs and tables are important because you cannot just read lists of numbers to people. After the third number you give them, they'll either be asleep or thinking of something else. They want to know the bottom line—now.

RUNDOWN >>

Using quantitative tools consists of three skills:

#29 USE NUMBERS

means applying mathematical and statistical tools in everyday life.

#30 USE GRAPHS AND TABLES

Using graphs and tables means creating visual representations of data from a spreadsheet.

#31 USE SPREADSHEET PROGRAMS

Using spreadsheet programs means recording and analyzing information electronically.

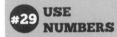

SKILLS WIN! ASSESSMENT

Take the following assessment for Skill Set #8. Put a check in the box next to each question. Make sure you answer the questions honestly. If you lie, you are lying to yourself and are probably hopeless.

Are you able to make simple calculations in your head?

- ☐ 1. I use a calculator for everything.
- ☐ 2. I can do calculations as long as it doesn't involve division.
- ☐ 3. I can do simple calculations in my head easily.

Can you calculate a percent change?

- ☐ 1. I am not sure what that is.
- ☐ 2. If you gave me the formula I could probably figure it out.
- ☐ 3. Yes, no problem.

Can you use numbers to provide evidence and strengthen an argument?

- ☐ 1. I've never done that before.
- ☐ 2. Occasionally, but not often.
- ☐ 3. Yes, I use numbers to strengthen my arguments all the time.

Do you know how to create a graph using information from a table?

1. No, I've done that before.
2. it may take me sometime, but I could figure it out.
3. Yes, I do that all the time.

Can you determine when to use different types of graphs? (line graph over a bar graph)

1. No.
2. Sometimes I'm unsure which will be the most effective.
3. Yes.

Are you able to use graphs to help prove a point in an argument?

1. Never done that before.
2. Some times.
3. Always.

Have you ever used a spreadsheet program like Excel?

1. No.
2. I know some basic functions, but I'm not proficient.
3. Yes, I use it for work all the time.

Given raw data, would you be able to create a spreadsheet to organize the information?

1. No.
2. If it wasn't an overwhelming amount of dat1.
3. No problem.

Can you create graphs and tables from a spreadsheet?

1. No.
2. Maybe a bar graph, but nothing too complex.
3. Yes, I can create all types of graphs and pivot tables too.

WHAT'S YOUR SKILLS WIN! SCORE?

Add the numbers you marked. See the table below to determine the number of stars.

Record your initial SkillsWin! score here:

_____

It is recommended that you return and take the assessment every three months. Space is provided below for you to record your SkillsWin! assessment score.

DATE   **SCORE**

_____   _____

_____   _____

_____   _____

_____   _____

SKILL #29
USE NUMBERS

Using numbers means applying mathematical and statistical tools in everyday life.

Using numbers means applying mathematical and statistical tools in everyday life. If you do not know why the statement "everyone in this city is above average" is nonsense, you have a lot of work to do in developing a minimum competence in the use of numbers. Make sure you have the ability to (1) calculate and interpret percentages, (2) use simple statistical terms like average, range, and correlation, (3) put together a budget, and above all, (4) have a healthy skepticism when numbers are thrown at you. No matter what your job is, you need to calculate in your head what it means when your boss tells you that you are getting a five percent raise next year. Your performance will be measured in numbers just as the performance of your company or agency is measured in the number of sales, the amount of income, or the number of people served. For most jobs, you don't have to be a mathematical whiz, but you do need to be able to add, subtract, multiply, divide, calculate percentages, solve simple equations, and interpret simple graphs.

BE A WINNER!

If you are one of those number-phobic people who says "I can't do math," you may not be as challenged as you think you are. It never ceases to amaze me how quickly number-phobic people can calculate, in a flash, the amount of money saved from a 40 percent sale.

Many activities that you might enjoy would improve your number skills. Shopping is one example, especially if you start figuring how out much your use of credit will cost you or if you are purchasing a car and need a loan. Sports statistics is an enjoyable way for sports fanatics to practice using numbers. Following the stock market can also make exercising math skills fun. Most importantly, you should be able to use these calculations to help you make decisions.

THINK ABOUT IT

How well do you use numbers? Circle your score.

1   **2**   **3**   **4**   **5**

POOR   OUTSTANDING

Comment on why you gave yourself this score here:

_____

_____

_____

_____

GAME CHANGERS

1 Become a treasurer of an organization with a real budget.

2 Exercise math skills with stock market values or sports information.

3 Calculate the percent difference in your income between the last two years.

MAKE A SKILL IMPROVEMENT PLAN

Describe and give clear examples of how you plan to improve or maintain how well you use numbers.

_____

_____

_____

_____

_____

_____

SKILL #30
USING GRAPHS AND TABLES

Using graphs and tables means creating visual representations of data from a spreadsheet.

You probably already know how to use simple graphs like bar and pie charts, and simple tables that show how numbers are related to each other. While the mechanics are easy, many people are not used to analyzing graphs and charts to make a point about a problem or decision that they face.

Whatever job you take will require you to analyze numbers and present them. Graphs and tables are important for presenting data because you cannot just read lists of numbers to people. They'll either be asleep or thinking of something else by the third number you give them. People are busy and want to know the bottom line—now. A carefully constructed graph or table that clearly illustrates a problem facing the organization (or better yet, a possible solution to the problem) will gain you considerable credit and help you move to the top quicker.

BE A WINNER

I am sure you have heard the phrase "a picture is worth a thousand words." The same principle applies to showing a series of numbers to someone. In this case, "a graph is worth a thousand numbers."

An equally important reason that you should use graphs and tables well is that it will enable you to question others when they present a graph or table to you. Statistics are often displayed in a way that makes them somewhat misleading. For this reason, attention to detail is also very important when using graphs and tables, especially when percentages are provided. For example, if a graph is comparing percentages of genders at a specific college, you should know that the two bars for male and female must add up to 100%. If you never thought of this, you need to practice this skill immediately.

THINK ABOUT IT

How well do you use graphs and tables? Circle your score.

1   **2**   **3**   **4**   **5**

POOR   OUTSTANDING

Comment on why you gave yourself this score here:

_____

_____

_____

_____

GAME CHANGERS

1 Recreate a graph of your expenses and income for the last three years.

2 Create two graphs that are different but have the same information.

3 Create a graph to project your income over the next three years and explain it to a friend or family member.

MAKE A SKILL IMPROVEMENT PLAN

Describe and give clear examples of how you plan to improve or maintain how well you use graphs and tables.

_____

_____

_____

_____

_____

_____

SKILL #31
USE SPREADSHEET PROGRAMS

Using spreadsheet programs means recording and analyzing information electronically.

Spreadsheets are equally as important to the analysis of information as a map is to getting to Grandma's house. Spreadsheets create order and simplify huge amounts of complex information so that you can make decisions.

If you don't even know what spreadsheet programs are, don't worry. You can easily understand the basics. A spreadsheet program helps you order information into lists and charts, conduct statistical analyses, and make graphs. The only spreadsheet software you will need to know is Microsoft Excel, the spreadsheet of choice for most business, government, and nonprofit organizations. Spreadsheets can be used to organize documents that contain numerous pieces of information, like mailing lists. Spreadsheets can also be used to generate statistics, tables, and graphs.

Being able to organize information into lists and tables and knowing how to compile and present statistics is becoming an increasingly important part of most jobs, particularly at the entry level. Solid Excel skills will get you in the door and make your boss forever grateful. Since spreadsheet programs are so widely used, temp firms are constantly looking for individuals to enter data for their clients. This means you can get a higher paying part-time job from a temp firm—much more than you would get parking cars or working in a fast food restaurant. Even if you are in a physical labor job at a fast food restaurant or construction company, using Excel can get you into a management position. The opportunities to find employment and advance in your career are practically endless if you can demonstrate that you have solid Excel skills. Using spreadsheets is also critical in the worlds of non-profit and government work in addition to business.

BE A WINNER!

One of my recent graduates who works at a large corporation and is about as far from a computer nerd as anyone can be, wrote me the following: "I will deny this if you repeat it, but I totally underestimated your emphasis on Excel. It is slowly becoming my best friend. Lately I've had dreams about how to improve my pivot tables and use V-lookups." I had preached to her, as I do to everyone I try to help that, EXCEL IS LIFE.

THINK ABOUT IT

How well do you use spreadsheet programs? Circle your score.

1　　**2**　　**3**　　**4**　　**5**

POOR　　　　　　　　　　　　　　OUTSTANDING

Comment on why you gave yourself this score here:

_____

_____

_____

_____

GAME CHANGERS

1 Create a table of the high temperatures for this past month in your area. Calculate the high, low, mean, median, and mode by using the Excel table tools.

2 Watch three Excel tutorials online.

3 Make a spreadsheet and bar graph with gender demographics of a group you belong to.

MAKE A SKILL IMPROVEMENT PLAN

Describe and give clear examples of how you plan to improve or maintain how well you use spreadsheet programs.

_____

_____

_____

_____

_____

_____

_____

SKILL SET #9

ASKING AND ANSWERING THE RIGHT QUESTIONS

The four skills in this chapter are collectively referred to by most people as "critical-thinking skills."

Employers say they want their employees to have these skills, and if you ask them to give you examples of "critical thinking," they usually identify one or more of the four skills in this skills set. They want you to be able to see through a salesperson's rhetoric, check for mistakes while recording information, answer any question with the right amount of detail, find information required to make a decision, and present it clearly or comment on the success or failure of an idea. Employers also want you to be good at evaluating yourself and evaluating others' ideas and behaviors and problem solving, which will be discussed in Chapter 10.

RUNDOWN >>

Asking and answering the right questions consists of four skills:

#32 DETECT NONSENSE

means questioning the accuracy of information that is presented as factual, whether it comes from people, institutions, or the media.

#33 PAY ATTENTION TO DETAIL

means being precise and accurate in answering questions, creating documents, records and projects, and making decisions.

#34 APPLY KNOWLEDGE

means using the information you have to reach conclusions and make informed decisions.

#35 EVALUATE ACTIONS AND POLICIES

means being able to identify, measure, and evaluate the success and failure of goals.

SKILLS WIN! ASSESSMENT

Take the following assessment for Skill Set #9. Put a check in the box next to each question. Make sure you answer the questions honestly. If you lie, you are lying to yourself and probably will not succeed as you would like.

After reading through an information packet would you:
☐ 1. Take it as truth.
☐ 2. Question some of the information but generally believe it.
☐ 3. Always look for questionable or selective facts, or broad generalizations that have obvious exceptions.

Do you consider bias when collecting and determining the legitimacy of information?
☐ 1. Not really.
☐ 2. Sometimes, especially if it is really obvious bias.
☐ 3. Always look for biases.

Do you check yourself for nonsense when you say or write things?
☐ 1. No because I never say anything without backing it up.
☐ 2. I know I should be more careful but frequently get carried away on rants.
☐ 3. I am always conscious of the need to check myself with examples when making generalizations.

Do you read directions multiple times before completing a task?
☐ 1. Once is enough.
☐ 2. I'll read all the way through once and then skim them afterwards.
☐ 3. At least two times before starting and then multiple times throughout the process.

When copying quotes from a source to a memo or paper, do you:
☐ 1. Cut and paste or type without checking.
☐ 2. Sometimes reread what I pasted or copied, by reading it over but not against the original.
☐ 3. Always, because I know how easy it is to drop part of the quote or make a typo.

When scheduling on a calendar or quoting a number or dollar amount, do you:
☐ 1. Depending on your memory.
☐ 2. Sometimes double check the information.
☐ 3. Always, double check.

How would you decide if you needed knowledge for something you were saying or writing?
☐ 1. Only if I were in school.
☐ 2. If I think my view might be challenged, I would seek knowledge but otherwise I am sure that I always think things out well.
☐ 3. Never want to reinvent the wheel so I conduct web searches and confer with experts to make sure I can gain from existing information.

Using knowledge that I find for decisions is:
☐ 1. Pretty easy.
☐ 2. Can be difficult; just takes a little time.
☐ 3. Is very difficult and time consuming and usually requires some background knowledge.

When do you consider outside knowledge important?
- ☐ 1. Rarely because I am usually faced with unique decisions.
- ☐ 2. Sometimes it is useful but I am too busy to give it the time it needs unless required by my boss.
- ☐ 3. I always ask myself, "Can I find some information that will help me make the decision?"

When making a decision or assessing the actions or policies of others, do you clearly identify goals?
- ☐ 1. I always have goals in mind but rarely state them clearly to myself or others.
- ☐ 2. Occasionally I will write goals and discuss them with others before I make a decision.
- ☐ 3. Yes, you need to be able to identify clear goals.

Are you able to measure goals, success and failure?
- ☐ 1. No because you know when you are successful.
- ☐ 2. Only if I need to prove to someone that I am successful.
- ☐ 3. I believe if you can't somehow measure your success or failure, you are not clear about your goals.

How can you tell if your decision is better than another one you could have taken?
- ☐ 1. You can't because you can't predict things that are hypothetical.
- ☐ 2. Think about what might have been better to do.
- ☐ 3. I ask others to judge what I did against what I might have done.

WHAT'S YOUR SKILLS WIN! SCORE?

Add the numbers you marked. See the table below to determine the number of stars.

.5	1	1.5	2	2.5	3	3.5	4	4.5	5
12-14	15-17	18-20	21-23	24-26	27-28	29-30	31-32	33-34	35-36
⇂	★	★⇂	★★	★★⇂	★★★	★★★⇂	★★★★	★★★★★	★★★★★

Record your initial SkillsWin! score here:

_____

It is recommended that you return and take the assessment every three months. Space is provided below for you to record your SkillsWin! assessment score.

DATE   **SCORE**

_____   _____

_____   _____

_____   _____

_____   _____

SKILL #32
DETECT NONSENSE

Detecting nonsense means questioning the accuracy of information that is presented as factual whether it comes from people, institutions, or the media.

Being able to detect nonsense is critical to your job success. Whatever job you take will require finding the correct information about the tasks you need to perform and the conditions that affect your performance. This information often comes from written sources, as well as statements from your boss, coworkers, those you serve, and others.

The reason that you should always be in "nonsense detection mode" when you hear or read anything is because information is always generated with a purpose, and unfortunately that purpose often gets in the way of the truth. You know this from your behavior, unless you have never told a little white lie or a big one. People tend to say what they think others want to hear. You don't trust advertisers to tell the truth. Well everyone is in "advertising mode" to some extent and sometimes they don't even know it. When it comes to detecting nonsense, you need to do two things. First, when reading or listening to other people, ask yourself if the person is consistent in what they say. If they change numbers when describing sales or price, you should start to worry about the whole conversation.

The second key to good nonsense detection is having as much knowledge as you can on the topic. Having a broad range of background knowledge can help you detect nonsense. If someone says something that you know is inaccurate, you can ask some questions to see how much the person doesn't know. If that happens a couple of times with that person, you can raise your nonsense detection radar on everything he or she says. Watch out for people who make general statements but when you ask for statistics, they give you one example.

BE A WINNER!

Your boss is likely to be a good nonsense detector. He asks how you are feeling today. You may not be well because you didn't get enough sleep. You may say "fine" because you want your boss to think you are in great shape for the workday. If your boss has a strong nose for nonsense, he may ask some more questions and find out you are not really ready for work.

THINK ABOUT IT

How well do you detect nonsense? Circle your score.

1　　**2**　　**3**　　**4**　　**5**

POOR　　　　　　　　　　　　　　　OUTSTANDING

Comment on why you gave yourself this score here:

_____

_____

_____

_____

GAME CHANGERS

1 Conduct research by comparing three cars or colleges.

2 Ask questions about the source of the information when people make a factual statement.

3 Be suspicious of all generalizations.

MAKE A SKILL IMPROVEMENT PLAN

Describe and give clear examples of how you plan to improve or maintain how well you detect nonsense.

_____

_____

_____

_____

_____

_____

SKILL #33
PAY ATTENTION TO DETAIL

Paying attention to detail means being precise and accurate in answering questions, creating documents, records, and projects, and making decisions.

In whatever task you undertake, you must get as many details correct as possible. You need to be like a medical doctor, piecing the sequence of events together and creating a pattern in your mind that helps you determine the reasons for the event. Can you, in effect, create a story that explains why a patient is ill, why a client did not buy your services, why a student failed a course, or why a person you supervise did the wrong thing?

Paying attention to detail will help you answer critical questions that could catapult you to the top of your career. Ignoring the details and the questions could result in a pink slip. Why does the boss keep criticizing you? What accounts for the sale of one item instead of another? Why does an individual praise or attack your organization? The answer to all of these questions often demands a strong focus on details.

An alumnus who has a very successful career in the federal government sent this bit of advice to my students: "you may think five points for turning in a paper late or two points here and there for formatting is silly or bothersome. Guess what? There's an entire section of the Federal Acquisition Regulation, which governs federal contracts, that specifically speaks to formatting, deadlines, and the consequences. Not following the rules can get a multi-million dollar proposal thrown out without the evaluator reading page one! No excuses, no second chances. Try explaining to your employer that you just lost revenue dollars and jobs because you didn't use the right-sized margins or font. Two points doesn't seem so frivolous now, does it?"

BE A WINNER!

How would you like to be a university administrator who put an ad in the newspaper for a program and listed an incorrect phone number, which just happened to be the number of a phone sex line? Probably not!

THINK ABOUT IT

How well do you pay attention to detail? Circle your score.

1   **2**   **3**   **4**   **5**

POOR   OUTSTANDING

Comment on why you gave yourself this score here:

_____

_____

_____

_____

GAME CHANGERS

1 Proofread everything: e-mails, papers, text messages, and class notes.

2 Give someone directions on how to do a math problem or how to find your way home.

3 Notice the name of every street you pass on the way to or from school and work.

MAKE A SKILL IMPROVEMENT PLAN

Describe and give clear examples of how you plan to improve or maintain your attention to detail.

_____

_____

_____

_____

_____

_____

SKILL #34
APPLY KNOWLEDGE

Applying knowledge means using the information you have to reach conclusions and make informed decisions.

The famous quote "knowledge is power" is not quite correct. Knowledge is a source of power, but knowledge is powerful only if it is used effectively. The usefulness of the knowledge you find or develop requires you to continually ask yourself, "What does this mean for my job and my organization?" The ability to get key statistics, find people who have the knowledge you need, and be alert to current trends in your field can help you in whatever job you have. Outstanding employees always look for the "best practices" that they can apply to their problems. You also need to be aware of "bad" and "mediocre practices" so you can avoid the mistakes others have made. Knowledge about what other organizations have done can help your organization and therefore you career.

Whatever job you have will require you to be committed to acquiring new knowledge throughout your career. Research does not stop after graduation for true Skills Winners. You'll need to keep up with publications in your field, go to professional meetings, and translate the general knowledge that is relevant to your specific job. If studies related to your job exist, you will need to apply the principles of the scientific method to make judgments about how much faith you can put in those studies. You will also need to learn how to decide which sources can be trusted. Having an eagerness and a curiosity to learn about all aspects of your job field is the holy grail of success.

BE A WINNER!

A successful insurance underwriter explains why he is always searching for new knowledge in his field. He says that he was able to move up through organizations quickly, and possibly higher than others (even those with advanced degrees), because of his commitment to searching for information during all waking hours. He is always looking for new information as it relates to my field. "This allows me to be in control of the success or failure of my career. It also puts me at a competitive advantage personally, as I become a more valued 'asset' of my organization, rather than another face in the crowd."

THINK ABOUT IT

How well do you apply knowledge? Circle your score.

1	**2**	**3**	**4**	**5**
POOR				OUTSTANDING

Comment on why you gave yourself this score here:

_____

_____

_____

_____

GAME CHANGERS

1 Create a table of the high temperatures for this past month in your area. Calculate the high, low, mean, median, and mode by using the Excel table tools.

2 Watch three Excel tutorials Online.

3 Make a spreadsheet and bar graph with gender demographics of a group to which you belong.

MAKE A SKILL IMPROVEMENT PLAN

Describe and give clear examples of how you plan to improve or maintain how well you apply knowledge.

_____

_____

_____

_____

_____

_____

SKILL #35
EVALUATE ACTIONS AND POLICIES

Evaluating actions and policies means being able to identify, measure, and evaluate the success and failure of goals.

You cannot avoid the challenge of evaluating your own performance and the performance of others. Unfortunately, evaluating is a task that produces anxiety. Most students who do not like tests will get sweaty palms before receiving a paper grade. Most people in the work world have a similar response when they hear the words "performance review." The anxiety comes from the combination of the excitement of winning or the fear of losing in one's career.

People develop many clever ways to avoid evaluation. They may blame others or take actions that are "safe." They may procrastinate. If they are confronted with a failure, they go into a depression and blame themselves. If they decide they have been successful, they may conclude that they are a winner and can do no wrong. To make matters worse, people who should be evaluating others will "hold their tongue" so they don't find themselves in a confrontation or they don't threaten the person's self-esteem. These behaviors need to be avoided if you wish to develop a capacity to evaluate your own actions and the actions of others.

This process is critical for the world of work. By continually asking yourself "how am I doing?" you improve your job performance. By asking how your unit is doing or company as a whole is doing, you contribute to a team effort to do the best.

Evaluation skills are essential for improving the performance of your organization. You will be a better employee if you can help your organization focus on clear goals, measure performance according to those goals, and draw conclusions that will lead to future improvement.

BE A WINNER!

To be successful in the work world you need to distinguish between two types of evaluation. The first is evaluation to improve performance, and the second is to punish or reward you or others. The former is the most important over the long run and is part of what businesses call "continuous improvement." The latter can cause a lot of trouble, but it is used in most organizations as a major tool of promoting excellence. An organization that uses evaluation only as a reward or punishment is not a good place to work.

THINK ABOUT IT

How well do you evaluate actions and policies? Circle your score.

1 **2** **3** **4** **5**

POOR   OUTSTANDING

Comment on why you gave yourself this score here:

_____

_____

_____

_____

GAME CHANGERS

1 Spend some time debriefing or talking to your teammates after a project about what went well and what could have been better.

2 Compare your grade goals from the beginning of a course to your actual grades at the end of a semester.

3 Identify a goal you plan to achieve in the next month and after the month. Write down if you achieved your goal and what you might have done better.

MAKE A SKILL IMPROVEMENT PLAN

Describe and give clear examples of how you plan to improve or maintain your ability to evaluate actions and policies.

_____

_____

_____

_____

_____

_____

SKILL SET #10
SOLVING PROBLEMS

Effective problem solving starts with an attitude that asks "why not?" Why can't we do a better job? Problem solvers are into continuous improvement. Problem solving is much more than just pushing around a lot of information. It requires you to use information to form a plan of action and then to make decisions and take action, or talk to others who can help you implement the solution.

The problem-solving Skill Set builds on all nine Skill Sets previously discussed. It requires strong motivation, good communication skills, excellent people skills, and good research and analysis skills. In addition, a problem solver must be willing to take risks and to think about the big picture. The willingness to see problems and do something about them is critical for a successful career.

Employers rarely explicitly list problem solving as a key skill, but they do frequently mention critical thinking, initiative, adaptability, and leadership. These terms are frequently associated with the employees' willingness to improve themselves and their organization. Employers want workers who are optimistic about change. They want to hire employees who, in the words of one employer, "know how big the problem is, its frequency, and how long it will take to solve." Willingness to recognize and provide evidence of problems helps your boss quickly understand what needs to be addressed, which makes him or her ready to listen to your suggestions. Your interviewer may not use the term "problem solving," but he will be looking for it throughout your interview.

RUNDOWN >>

Solving Problems consists of three skills:

#36 IDENTIFY PROBLEMS

means knowing how to define a problem and how to provide evidence to support the problem's existence.

#37 DEVELOP SOLUTIONS

means creating a solution to eliminate a problem or reduce its negative effects.

#38 LAUNCH SOLUTIONS

means effectively implementing a plan or policy to solve or reduce a problem.

SKILLS WIN! ASSESSMENT

Take the following assessment for Skill Set #10. Put a check in the box next to each question. Make sure you answer the questions honestly. If you lie, you are lying to yourself and are probably hopeless.

Are you able to identify when there is a problem?
- ☐ 1. Not really.
- ☐ 2. Sometimes.
- ☐ 3. Always.

How will you know if you identified a problem?
- ☐ 1. When I feel that I have identified the problem.
- ☐ 2. When others agree with me that there is a problem.
- ☐ 3. When others agree with me that there is a problem and I have data to back it up.

You are at work and your colleague tells you that nothing will print, you are most likely to:
- ☐ 1. Tell her to ask the service department.
- ☐ 2. Try to print something from your computer and if it does not work, tell them to ask someone else.
- ☐ 3. Open the printer tray, make sure there is enough paper and ink, and double-check that she is printing to the correct printer.

How do you determine what the best solution is?
- ☐ 1. The first is always the best.
- ☐ 2. Brainstorming with others usually gets you the best solution.
- ☐ 3. Carefully weigh the benefits and costs of the solution.

Are you able to create reasonable and practical solutions?
- ☐ 1. My solutions are creative, but not practical.
- ☐ 2. They work, but are maybe not the most reasonable.
- ☐ 3. I have to think about who would support and who would oppose the solution.

How do you generate ideas for a solution?
- ☐ 1. Time and thought.
- ☐ 2. Getting other people's ideas and experiences.
- ☐ 3. Researching and learning as much as possible about the problem and basic solutions.

Once you have created a solution, how do you implement it?
- ☐ 1. Hand it off to someone else.
- ☐ 2. Create a list of everything that needs to be done.
- ☐ 3. Develop a strategy and come up with resources needed to aid in implementation.

How often are you able to get a solution implemented?
- ☐ 1. Rarely.
- ☐ 2. Sometimes it occurs but I don't know why except that it was a good idea.
- ☐ 3. Frequently, because I am willing to listen to others and make compromise.

What do you do to get your solution accepted?
- ☐ 1. Develop a really good idea.
- ☐ 2. See who supports it and encourage them to support the idea.
- ☐ 3. Make a list of people who will support or oppose them and then work to increase support and reduce opposition.

WHAT'S YOUR SKILLS WIN! SCORE?

Add the numbers you marked. See the table below to determine the number of stars.

.5	1	1.5	2	2.5	3	3.5	4	4.5	5
9-10	11-12	13-14	15-16	17-18	19-20	21-22	23-24	25-26	27
✦	★	★✦	★★	★★	★★	★★	★★	★★★	★★★
				✦	★	★✦	★★	★✦	★★

Record your initial SkillsWin! score here:

_____

It is recommended that you return and take the assessment every three months. Space is provided below for you to record your SkillsWin! assessment score.

DATE   **SCORE**

_____   _____

_____   _____

_____   _____

_____   _____

SKILL #36
IDENTIFY PROBLEMS

Identifying problems means knowing how to define a problem and how to provide evidence to support the problem's existence.

Any organization you work for has goals associated with its mission that are intended to help a company get the most out of its resources. Many problems arise when the mission is not being accomplished efficiently or at all. As an employee, you should want to "fix" or reduce the negative effect of these problems.

The first and most critical step in problem solving is to be clear about the nature of the problem. Identifying a problem is more than just saying one exists. It also requires evidence that demonstrates the problem is real. You may use statistical evidence showing the increase in time it takes between the ordering and the shipping of the goods in a chart. You may use a survey to show the frequency of customer complaints. You may simply decide to show that everyone in your unit agrees that there is a problem.

The key is substantiating in concrete terms that a problem exists, even before discussing solutions. Let's say the executive committee of a senior citizens' center decides that more publicity is needed to attract more people to their facilities. The committee will get into arguments about how best to publicize their center, without first understanding the real problem in this case is the lack of participation. If they look at lack of participation as the problem, maybe they would realize that the real cause may be the lack of attractive programs and not the lack of public relations. A problem-solving orientation will help you avoid this trap.

Identifying the problem in such a way that the definition of it is clear and that some evidence is available that it actually exists, requires skills in working with people, information gathering, verbal and written communication, and quantitative analysis. Above all, it requires asking and answering the right questions. Once you have documented the problem, you are ready to search for the major causes of the problem which in turn will help you discover solutions.

BE A WINNER!

The famous saying "don't kill the messenger" applies to identifying the problem. Most leaders don't like to hear bad news especially if it reflects what they or their unit is doing. Other colleagues may also get mad. You need to think about the consequences of calling attention to the problem or defining it in a certain way. That is why it is so important to have clear evidence. Equally important, is getting a few other people to agree with you on the problem. Even so, you could get in trouble.

THINK ABOUT IT

How well do you identify problems? Circle your score.

1 **2** **3** **4** **5**

POOR   OUTSTANDING

Comment on why you gave yourself this score here:

_____

_____

_____

_____

GAME CHANGERS

1 Make a list of potential problems you see for the week. Write why they are problems for you or someone else.

2 When you're in meetings be sure to Repeatedly ask: "what's the problem(s)?" until everyone agrees on the same problem(s).

3 Be sure to answer the question: "Who is this a problem for?"

MAKE A SKILL IMPROVEMENT PLAN

Describe and give clear examples of how you plan to improve or maintain how well you identify problems.

_____

_____

_____

_____

_____

_____

SKILL #37
DEVELOP SOLUTIONS

Developing solutions means creating a solution to eliminate a problem or reduce its negative effects.

Once you have identified a problem, the next step is to come up with possible solutions. Our definition makes clear that "solutions" is too strong a word in many cases. Difficult and persistent problems, especially ones that involve many people, are never solved. These kinds of problems are not physical ones like a dripping faucet, which can be fixed. Problem solving is frequently about reducing the negative effects of a problem and not necessarily eliminating its causes. In medicine, you can treat a cough of unknown origins with cough syrup, to reduce the severity of the symptom, but you may never treat the underlying cause of the cough. Solutions in every field can either treat the symptoms or the cause. Sometimes if the symptom goes away, the causes will eventually go away. In the business world, your competitors' products and advertising are frequently the primary underlying cause of your poor sales. You cannot eliminate the competitors, but you can improve your product or advertising to win back sales. A preferred solution would be to put your competitors out of business, but that rarely happens.

BE A WINNER

Many bosses want you to bring problems to them. However, they also want you to propose a solution to the problem as you present it. If you just bring the problem, you may be perceived as whining. If you bring a solution that provides clear evidence of the problem, it shows that you are into continuous improvement, which is every bosses dream.

Solutions may be found by looking at what others have done in similar situations as well as creating new solutions. When it comes to solving problems, research and creativity are both required. Researching what has been done to address this problem in the past means searching for both effective and failed practices. Applying those practices to your problems requires creating an action plan that adapts the idea to a new situation. If your research does not yield a relevant effective practice, you need to think up an idea on your own. Employers want you to always be thinking about ways of solving problems that you, your department, and your organization face.

THINK ABOUT IT

How well do you develop solutions? Circle your score.

1	2	3	4	5
POOR				OUTSTANDING

Comment on why you gave yourself this score here:

_____

_____

_____

_____

GAME CHANGERS

1 Once you have identified a problem, brainstorm with a group to come up with the best ideas for a solution.

2 Make a list of pros and cons for possible solutions and their consequences when making a decision.

3 Make sure that you know and understand the different causes of the problems.

MAKE A SKILL IMPROVEMENT PLAN

Describe and give clear examples of how you plan to improve or maintain how well you develop solutions.

_____

_____

_____

_____

_____

_____

_____

SKILL #38
LAUNCH SOLUTIONS

Launching solutions means effectively implementing a plan or policy to solve or reduce a problem.

After you have clearly identified the problem and settled on a solution you think will work (at least partially), you face the most difficult and frustrating part of problem solving: implementing the solution. Solutions, by definition, create change, and people typically resist change because they fear the unknown and are afraid they will personally lose something (like their job or a promised raise). The first and most important skill in launching solutions is to be able to anticipate resistance to change and implement an effective strategy anyway.

Start by soliciting the opinions of others in an effort to create solutions. Part of the creative process is soliciting reactions to your initial ideas and then adjusting to legitimate criticism. Realize that creating a solution alone is never as effective as creating a solution through mutual exchange. You will have to make compromises to adjust to ideas suggested by others or overcome roadblocks that get in the way.

BE A WINNER!

A typical interview question is "What decision or action are you most proud of?" You will impress your potential employer if you can provide a story of how you identified a problem and worked with others to come up with a solution, even if it was only partially successful. One of my students landed a high-paying job when he told the interviewer how he decided that kids in a small community center located in a housing project needed computers and that he was later able to obtain eight used computers for the center.

Launching solutions requires you to get the problem and the solution on the agenda of those who have the power. Those who have power are busy, and although they say they want solutions, they usually want them at no cost to themselves or their organization. Moreover, to get your solution on the table, you need to convince those above you that there is a very serious problem. Doing this without offending those responsible is no easy task. Finally, build support amongst your co-workers so that your solution is seriously considered. Building support requires getting others to buy into the idea: the more powerful your supporters, the better.

All 37 other skills will play a role in your success at launching solutions, which is why it usually leads to promotions. People who solve problems reach higher levels in their career for two reasons: problem-solving is highly valued by employers, and there is a short supply of people who can successfully problem-solve.

THINK ABOUT IT

How well do you launch solutions? Circle your score.

1   **2**   **3**   **4**   **5**

POOR   OUTSTANDING

Comment on why you gave yourself this score here:

_____

_____

_____

_____

GAME CHANGERS

1 Organize a to-do list that prioritizes your actions and answers the questions: Where are we now? Where do we want to be? How do we get there?

2 Write a list of measurable goals to help accomplish your solutions.

3 Create a list of milestones you will reach during your solution's implementation process.

MAKE A SKILL IMPROVEMENT PLAN

Describe and give clear examples of how you plan to improve or maintain your ability to launch solutions.

_____

_____

_____

_____

_____

_____